Engaging the Closed Minded

Presenting Your Faith to the Confirmed Unbeliever

Dan Story

kregel
PUBLICATIONS

Grand Rapids, MI 49501

Engaging the Closed Minded: Presenting Your Faith to the Confirmed Unbeliever

© 1999 by Dan Story

Published by Kregel Publications, a division of Kregel, Inc., P.O. Box 2607, Grand Rapids, MI 49501. Kregel Publications provides trusted, biblical publications for Christian growth and service. Your comments and suggestions are valued.

For more information about Kregel Publications, visit our web site: www.kregel.com

Cover photos: © PhotoDisc
Cover design: Nicholas G. Richardson
Book design: Kevin Ingram

Library of Congress Cataloging-in-Publication Data
Story, Dan.
Engaging the closed minded: presenting your faith to the confirmed unbeliever / Dan Story.
       p.   cm.
   1. Evangelistic work. 2. Apologetics. I. Title.
BV3793.S69   1999   269'.2—dc21   99-33787
                                           CIP

ISBN 0-8254-3677-x

Printed in the United States of America
1 2 3 4 5 / 03 02 01 00 99

Contents

To my friends and colleagues
at the Simon Greenleaf Center

Foreword

Dan Story received his M.A. in apologetics in the halcyon days of the Simon Greenleaf School of Law when it still offered an apologetics master's degree. The school's underlying philosophy, developed by Walter R. Martin, Harold Lindsell, and myself as founding dean, was to approach the defence of the faith from an *evidential* standpoint—much as a great trial lawyer will marshal his proofs and tailor his presentation so as to convince a jury and obtain the right verdict. Dan took to this approach like the proverbial duck to water, and in the intervening years he has made an impressive impact for Christ in the realm of popular apologetics. This book is a further testimony to his astuteness in offering a "reason for the hope that is within us" in terms that the typical Christian can understand and appreciate.

Why is this kind of book important? Because, in general, evangelical Christians do not do much effective apologetics. They are hampered by (1) a pietism that emphasises the heart over the head and sees any attempt at argument as probably unspiritual and unchristlike, and (2) the deleterious effects of "presuppositionalism," which claims that in a fallen world one can never convince an unbeliever of the correctness of the Christian position. But Dan well shows in this practical handbook that giving reasons for the faith is the essence of concerned, Spirit-motivated evangelism, and that one must deal with non-Christians in an open marketplace of ideas, not expect them to accept *ab initio* the truth of Christian revelation.

Dan's book focuses on the problem of the "closed minded"— those who have decided they will have nothing to do with Christianity. What does the concerned believer do with them? The pietist will pray for them; the presuppositionalist will preach to them—and both will then pass by on the other side. Dan, however, shows how to bind up their intellectual wounds and lead them evidentially to the "many infallible truths" of the eternal gospel of Christ.

I commend this book to those who want to carry out such a task in fulfilment of the Great Commission.

JOHN WARWICK MONTGOMERY, PH.D., TH.D.

Professor Emeritus of Law and Humanities,
University of Luton, England

Distinguished Professor of Apologetics,
Trinity College & Theological Seminary, Newburgh, Indiana

Distinguished Professor of Law, Regent University,
Virginia Beach, Virginia

Senior Counsel, European Centre for Law & Justice,
Strasbourg, France

Introduction

In the late 1970s, while living in San Diego, my wife and I became good friends with neighbors across the street. We had a lot in common: we were about the same age, our kids got along well, and we enjoyed playing games and going backpacking together.

The wife, I'll call her "Cindy," was a third-generation Christian Scientist. Her husband, "Jeff," I can best describe as an I-couldn't-care-less-about-religion secular humanist. At the time, I was pretty much an "Easter Sunday Christian" (that's normally when I attended church), and, as far as I knew, Christian Science was just another Christian denomination that liked science!

Eventually, both our families moved out of town. We moved to a rural community twenty-five miles away, and Jeff and Cindy moved to central California. A few years later, however, they returned to the San Diego area.

During the interim between our friends' move to central California and their return to San Diego, I became a Christian and returned to college, eventually earning a Master of Arts degree in Christian apologetics. So by the time Jeff and Cindy returned to Southern California, I knew that Christian Science was a cult—and I was eager for a *confrontation*.

The opportunity came one evening when we invited them over for supper. After eating we went outside to sit on our deck. I immediately unsheathed my apologetic sword and plunged into battle. The result was disastrous.

It wasn't that I failed to give a good account of myself. With little effort, I cut to shreds Cindy's erroneous beliefs. I deftly pared her objections to Christianity while skillfully slicing away her defenses of Christian Science. She had no answers to my challenges, no rebuttal to my facts. I did my job, all right. In my mind's eye, she had to admit that, at best, she was simply deceived by an inane cult, and, at worst, she was a naive buffoon.

She did neither. And we never heard from Cindy and Jeff again.

What went wrong? Obviously, the problem was me. It was a classic case of "winning the battle but losing the war." I had all the answers, but that only meant that I was half trained. What I lacked was gentleness (1 Peter 3:15b) and communication skills (2 Tim. 2:24–25). Had I used my apologetics sword properly, I would have pricked Cindy's conscience so that she would begin to question her religious worldview. But I would have done so gently, being careful not to inflict a mortal wound. Instead, I chased her away, bleeding and unconvinced.

My tactic was designed to win the argument, not the soul. I failed to create an environment in which the Holy Spirit was free to convict Cindy of the falsity of Christian Science, while at the same time convince her (and Jeff) of the truth of Christianity.

I share this story to illustrate an important principle of apologetics: Having the knowledge to intellectually combat and defeat non-Christian religions and philosophies is not enough. It's also necessary to debate these issues and to present the Christian perspective in such a way that unbelievers will listen and understand.

Teaching this is the purpose of this book, the third in a series of apologetics studies. My first book, *Defending Your Faith*,[1] answers the "tough" questions. It provides responses to the major questions and criticisms unbelievers raise against Christianity. My second book, *Christianity on the Offense*,[2] examines the other side of the apologetics coin. Instead of "defensive" apologetics, it presents "offensive" apologetics. It provides instructions on how to examine and test religious truth-claims. It challenges modern non-Christian worldviews, both religious and secular.

This book is a study on how to *apply* apologetics effectively as a tool for evangelism. It provides instructions on how to use apologetics data and techniques as an aid to evangelism. It provides practical training on how to shift the "burden of proof" from believers to unbelievers—where it belongs, since they are the ones entertaining untruths.

I believe that apologetics must be employed in evangelistic encounters more today than at anytime in church history. We live in a world that is *pluralistic* and *morally relativistic*.[3] Increasingly, people today accept all religious and philosophical worldviews as equally true and worthy of acceptance. Likewise, the majority of Americans believe that all moral behavior is acceptable as long as it doesn't "hurt anyone else." Ethics are not universal. Nor do they originate from a transcendent God who sets the standards of moral behavior and holds people accountable for how they behave.

This *post-Christian* and *postmodern* world holds to the premise that there are no absolute truths that apply to everyone equally. Christianity and Christian ethics are no longer relevant. In fact, orthodox Christians are seen as bigoted, narrow-minded, and anti-intellectual because we refuse to accept other religions as "paths to God" or to consider homosexuality, pornography, or abortion as permissible in a moral society.

In light of the cultural war raging between Christians and non-Christians, it's crucial that all believers engage in evangelism—as our Lord directs in Acts 1:8. But to evangelize successfully in a pluralistic, morally relativistic, and postmodern world means that we must be prepared to share more than the gospel message. We must learn to defend our beliefs, to challenge the unbeliever's beliefs, and to demonstrate that Christianity is not only emotionally and spiritually satisfying but also relevant to modern culture.

Even more important, we must demonstrate that Christianity is *truth*. In other words, if God exists, and if He has revealed Himself to mankind, it is only through Christianity. There are no other options.

This book will focus on seven crucial apologetic tactics:

1. How to communicate our faith and apologetic data in a way that unbelievers will listen to us and give us a fair hearing.
2. How to respond to challenges and misconceptions concerning Christianity.
3. How to identify obstacles to faith in Jesus Christ as they surface during discussions with unbelievers.
4. How to challenge non-Christian beliefs and worldview assumptions; that is, how to put the "burden of proof" on unbelievers so that they are the ones who must explain what

they believe, why they believe it, and then justify it with compelling evidence (as they expect Christians to do).

5. How to argue (in a good sense) persuasively and logically so that we sound convincing and compelling.

6. How to control the conversation in apologetic or evangelistic encounters.

7. How to establish a "point of contact" with unbelievers—an area of mutual agreement that can be used as a springboard for evangelism.

This is a lot of ground to cover, but we'll do it. So let's get started.

Endnotes

1. Dan Story, *Defending Your Faith* (Grand Rapids: Kregel, 1997).
2. Dan Story, *Christianity on the Offense* (Grand Rapids: Kregel, 1998).
3. *Christianity on the Offense* explains the influence and prevalence of these modern social and religious philosophies and provides a Christian response.

1

Apologetics as Evangelism

Years ago I met, in church, a woman whose husband was an atheist. He was also a very talented musician, and occasionally he was invited to play his guitar during special church functions. Understandably, this created a controversy within the body. Because of his unbelief, many people in the congregation resented his participation in church-related musicals. They thought it was an affront to God to allow an avowed atheist to participate in music designed to lead the congregation in worshiping Him. Others disagreed. They argued that allowing him to perform in church was a form of witnessing. He would develop relationships with believers and hear the gospel preached.

As the controversy intensified, the pastor and I visited the family and got to know the husband better. He was a likable guy, and as we were leaving I invited him to have supper with me. I wanted some one-on-one time, hoping to discover the reason he was an atheist and to convince him otherwise.

This experience illustrates two approaches to evangelism. Together, they provide a witnessing format for every unbeliever you encounter—regardless of beliefs or reasons for rejecting Christianity.

The first approach is called *lifestyle* evangelism (see Matt. 5:16; John 13:35; Col. 4:5–6; 1 Peter 2:12). It stresses building relationships with unbelievers in order to provide witnessing opportunities. It's a long-term commitment, one where unbelievers are able to witness Christians modeling the Christian lifestyle.

The idea is this. Because Christians can experience a profound sense of peace during life's many crises, and because we have the power of God to deal with suffering and to resist sin, unbelievers can observe this and desire a similar relationship with Christ. Allowing the atheist to participate in church musicals so that he would have the opportunity to meet and develop friendships with Christians illustrates lifestyle evangelism.

The second approach to evangelism is referred to as *proclamation*. It entails verbally proclaiming either gospel, law, or apologetics (I'll define these terms in a moment).

In 2 Timothy 4:2 Paul exhorts believers to preach the Word. He also implicitly endorses the use of apologetics: "Preach the Word; be prepared in season and out of season; *correct, rebuke and encourage*—with great patience and careful instruction" (my emphasis).

The goal of proclamation is to present a clear statement of the essential Christian message to unbelievers, in particular, the plan of salvation. However, this goal may not be achieved on a first encounter. Often, unbelievers will raise objections that will have to be overcome before they will seriously consider a gospel presentation. This is when apologetics comes into play. The visit to the atheist at his home and my dinner invitation illustrate proclamation.

Lifestyle Evangelism

This is a book on apologetics, so we will not examine lifestyle evangelism in detail. But I do want to make a few comments relevant to apologetics. Apologetics can include long-term relationships with unbelievers. This requires applying the principles of lifestyle evangelism.

We must remember that we are asking unbelievers to change their entire view of reality—the fundamental way in which they see life. We are asking them to move from one worldview to another, to forfeit their basic beliefs and assumptions about religion and morality. This may take time. A relationship with a committed Christian can be vital in order for their questions to be answered and their doubts to be removed, and to help them rethink their former beliefs, goals, and aspirations.

We must also realize that as Christians, we are always on stage before unbelievers. Many people watch for opportunities to point out and criticize our failures. Paul warns in 2 Timothy 3:12 that "everyone who wants to live a godly life in Christ Jesus will be persecuted."

But non-Christians also watch to see how we respond to life's challenges. This can make a tremendous impact on unbelievers. If we demonstrate through our lifestyles that we possess an inner strength and peace of mind that the world can't offer, Christianity can become extremely appealing to people who have never been responsive to direct witnessing (proclamation).

The principle here is this: The life a Christian lives in the presence of an unbeliever acts as a preview to what an unbeliever will see his life becoming if he becomes a Christian. If we are legalistic, condemning, or self-righteous, a non-Christian will not want to become a Christian because that is what he will see himself becoming if he does.

For example, an untimely or thoughtless comment on smoking, drinking, or watching R-rated movies nearly always will slam the door on evangelism. It doesn't matter whether or not these behaviors are wrong. Even worse, if we live a life more in harmony with the secular world than with the kingdom of God, an unbeliever will judge all Christians as hypocrites and believe that he or she was right all along in rejecting Christianity.

The point is that many unbelievers will choose to accept or reject Christianity on the basis of what they see—not what they hear. Even if we are clumsy in sharing our faith, it is often what unbelievers observe that draws them to Christ. If our lives reflect Jesus, it can create an interest in Christianity and lead to opportunities to share the gospel at a later time.

I can use myself as an example. For nine years my family lived next door to a Christian couple who not only "talked the talk" but also lived a Christian lifestyle. When we first moved into the neighborhood, I thought I was a Christian. I believed in God. I occasionally went to church. But I didn't have a personal relationship with Jesus Christ. Observing my neighbors—not just listening to what they said—was a major force compelling me to attend church regularly and to eventually make a personal commitment to the Lord.

Lifestyle evangelism—by both the individual and the local church as a whole—can be a decisive factor in witnessing to unbelievers. However, one can't be saved without a knowledge of Jesus and His work of atonement (Rom. 10:14–15). Sooner or later all people will need to hear the gospel proclaimed.

Proclamation

Proclamation is usually thought of as proclaiming the gospel message—the "good news" of salvation and transformation through Jesus Christ (see Matt. 24:14; Mark 13:10; Luke 24:47; Eph. 1:13). However, for our purposes here, I'm enlarging that definition to include not only proclaiming the gospel but also proclaiming law and apologetics. In other words, proclamation, as we will use it, is any verbal declaration of, or defense of, the Christian worldview.

When it comes to evangelism, many Christians have tunnel vision. They assume that nearly everyone who rejects Christianity does so for moral reasons. People reject Christianity because they don't want to make the lifestyle changes they believe becoming a Christian demands.

To a certain extent, this is true. As Kreeft and Tacelli point out in their *Handbook of Christian Apologetics*, "The most powerful psychological *motive* for unbelief . . . is almost always moral rather than intellectual."[1]

However, it is equally true that many unbelievers reject Christianity for other perceived reasons. There are intellectual reasons ("Becoming a Christian is committing intellectual suicide"); emotional reasons ("God would never accept me after what I did!"); and spiritual reasons ("You can't be saved unless you . . ."). Whatever the reason, as Kreeft and Tacelli add, "It's important to know what is really going on in the soul of the person to whom apologetic arguments are addressed, and to know the irrational forces behind unbelief."[2]

Because most Christians believe that people reject Christianity for moral reasons, they see evangelism as more or less a formula. First, give your personal testimony. Second, share the plan of salvation (e.g., the "Four Spiritual Laws" or the "Roman Road to Salvation"). Third, if the unbeliever doesn't respond (because, after all, his *real* reason is moral), threaten him with damnation. Once this formula has been completed, most Christians feel they have done their duty in evangelism.

To these Christians, apologetics is unnecessary—or, more likely, they don't know what it is or how to apply it. They don't realize that in today's pluralistic, relativistic, and largely godless society, many people reject Christianity for intellectual reasons, not moral reasons (although intellectual arguments are often an excuse to justify immoral behavior). Many unbelievers have been taught that Christianity and all religions are myths, vestiges from our pre-scientific past, the product of (in)fertile human imagination, or self-delusion.

The problem with the formula approach to evangelism is that it will reach only a portion of unbelievers. It will only persuade those whom God has prepared to respond specifically to the gospel message at that point in time. But this includes only a segment of the people to whom we have opportunities to witness.

Many people are not at a point in their spiritual journey where they are willing to listen to, let alone respond to, the plan of salvation. They have other concerns that need to be dealt with first. In particular, there may be genuine intellectual obstacles. But whatever the issues, if we are not prepared to respond to a person's misconceptions, false beliefs, criticisms, insecurities, doubts, or skepticism, we will reach only a small portion of unbelievers.

The remainder of this chapter is designed to help Christian apologists formulate a witnessing strategy according to an unbeliever's particular (1) view of God, and (2) view of salvation, to find out (3) whether he or she needs to hear law, gospel, or apologetics, and to discern (4) the unbeliever's personality type.

Four Views of God

In evangelism and apologetics, you will encounter four kinds of non-Christians in terms of their beliefs (or disbeliefs) in God. Paul and other New Testament evangelists encountered these same four varieties in the first century.

In Acts 17:1–3 Paul witnesses, "as his custom was," to the Jews in Thessalonica. The first type of unbeliever, which both Paul and we encounter, are those who believe in the God of Scripture (or a close facsimile) but reject Jesus Christ as Lord and Savior in the

Christian sense—or have never met Him. Today this group includes not only Orthodox Jews but also Muslims, Unitarians, and some Christian cults.

Further in the chapter (vv. 16–22), Paul witnesses to the Gentiles in Athens. These people represent a second variety of unbelievers: those who are "religious," like the Greeks, but have no concept of, or reject, the one true (Christian) God. Today, this group includes all primitive, polytheistic, and pantheistic religions: Animism (tribal religions), Mormonism, Scientology, the Unification Church, UFO religions, witchcraft, Hinduism, Buddhism, New Age cults, and so on.

Today's religious scene also includes a large number of people who have no affiliation with any kind of religion at all: agnostics and atheists. Most likely Paul seldom encountered this variety of unbelievers because, as Stephen Neill points out, "Until recent times, it could be taken for granted that the vast majority of human beings, if they were not Christians, would be adherents of some identifiable religion."[3] Nevertheless, atheism did exist in biblical times. Psalm 14:1 teaches that only a fool says in his heart, "There is no God," confirming that atheism existed centuries before Christ. Today, this group includes secular humanists, communists, materialists, naturalists, many existentialists, and others who hold atheistic philosophies.

Finally, there is a fourth category of people. I want to spend more time on this group, and you may be surprised that I include it in a list of non-Christian types. Perhaps the apostle Paul was referring to this group of unbelievers in Titus 1:16 where he states, "They claim to know God, but by their actions they deny him."

I believe these people comprise a large segment of the so-called Christian population today, especially in the United States and Europe. I'm speaking here of people who claim to be Christians (and probably believe they are) and thus think they are saved, when in fact they are not Christians and are not saved.

These people identify themselves as Christians because they live in a country that (historically, at least) was predominately Christian. They are "Christian" by culture or upbringing but not by personal commitment. Because of their lifestyle, these people show no indication of being Christian in spite of their claims. In other words, although they think of themselves as Christian, they do not function within a Christian framework; they do not actively promote the Christian worldview; they do not give any indication by word or deed that they are believers. They seldom or never go to church. In short, they are more secular than Christian.

Although only the Lord knows their true relationship with Him, I believe these people need to hear the gospel message and need to make a personal commitment to Jesus Christ. We'll talk more about them shortly.

Four Views of Salvation

In addition to identifying four kinds of unbelievers in terms of their views of God, it is also helpful to recognize the distinct views of salvation to which these four groups adhere. I believe that all people worldwide can be grouped into one of four categories in terms of their perceptions of salvation. These views more or less parallel the four kinds of unbelievers above.

The first group of people believes in the God of Scripture but feels unworthy of salvation or ignorant of the way of salvation.

The second group of people worships non-Christian gods and thinks it's saved through other religions.

The third group does not believe in any kind of God at all, or thinks God's unknowable if He does exist, and hence rejects the concept of salvation. These are the agnostics and atheists.

The fourth group believes in the Christian concept of God but thinks it is good enough to merit salvation. In other words, people in this group believe God will accept them just as they are because they are basically good people. Many of them believe that Jesus is their "Savior" but show no indication by word or deed of having personally received Him or committed their lives to Him.

Applying Law, Gospel, or Apologetics

You may be wondering why it's helpful to lump potential converts into one of four groups. The reason is because it allows us to determine whether to focus our evangelism on law, gospel, or apologetics. In evangelism, we always apply one of the three.

Apologetics, of course, is defending the Christian faith. But let's pause a moment and define law and gospel.

In the Old Testament we see three varieties of law. First are moral laws. These were the ethical standards and principles by which the Israelites were to live. Second are ceremonial laws. These were the laws that regulated Israel's religious rituals. And the third are civil laws. These laws maintained order in Jewish society.

The kind of law that I'm concerned with here is moral law, the timeless ethical standards outlined in the Ten Commandments. (I will subsequently refer to moral law as "law.") These laws applied not only to the ancient Jews but also to all people of every generation up to the present hour. Why? Because law represents what God demands of all people in order to be saved. To put it another way, if it were possible for people to get into heaven on their own merits, law tells what they would have to do.

Gospel, however, tells us what God has done for us because we are *unable to fulfill the law*. It's the free gift of forgiveness and salvation through the work of Jesus Christ.

Let's see how law and gospel work together in evangelism. The Bible teaches that God demands that all people live according to the law that He has set before them. In fact, He attaches penalties for breaking the law (i.e., for sinning). The ultimate penalty is eternal separation from God (2 Thess. 1:9).

The problem is, no one is capable of keeping the whole law all the time. The Bible clearly states this in Romans chapters 1–3 and in Galatians chapter 3. The Old Testament makes the same claim. King Solomon says in 1 Kings 8:46, "There is no one who does not sin."

Fortunately for the human race, God knew that nobody could keep all the law all the time; that is, no one is capable of never sinning. In fact, according to the Bible, the primary purpose of the law is to define sin and to show that all people are sinners (see Rom. 7:7) and guilty before a holy and righteous God. People are unable to save themselves through their good works (see Gal. 2:16).

So God gave us the gospel, the "Good News" that Jesus Christ took the punishment we deserve for our failure (and inability) to obey the law (see Rom. 5:8). Because Jesus paid the price in full (6:23b), we have the opportunity to become reconciled to God and to receive the gift of eternal life. In short, the law condemns, but the gospel saves. The law points us to the gospel of Christ as our only hope of salvation (see 8:1).

Now let's apply law, gospel, and apologetics to the four groups of people in the two categories outlined above. The idea is to choose the evangelistic approach that best fits the need of the individual according to his position in these categories. We'll look at three biblical examples and three non-biblical examples.

Biblical Examples

John 4:4–26 recounts the story of Jesus talking with the Samaritan woman. This woman had been married five times and was living with yet another man (v. 17). How did Jesus deal with her? Did He point out her failure to obey the law? No. She knew she was a sinner (v. 29). Did Jesus use apologetics to defend His messiahship? No. When He claimed to be the Messiah (v. 26), the woman didn't challenge it. Instead, Jesus proclaimed the gospel. He offered the woman forgiveness—"living water" (vv. 10, 13–14). Scriptures records that many of the Samaritans believed because of the woman's testimony (v. 39).

Luke 18:18–25 recounts a conversation between Jesus and a rich ruler. The ruler asked Jesus what he must do to be saved. Jesus told him he must obey the law. The man claimed that he had done so since his youth. But Jesus pointed out that the ruler lacked one thing. He was unwilling to forsake his earthly wealth to gain "treasure in heaven" (v. 22). In other words, he fell short of earning salvation through his own good works. He did not keep all the law. Jesus' evangelistic approach to the rich ruler was to apply law. Gospel or apologetics were not needed in his case.

In Acts 17:16–34 Paul is in Athens. While waiting for Silas and Timothy to join him, Paul was invited to speak to the Greek philosophers before the Areopagus. Paul's evangelistic strategy was to apply apologetics. The evidence he mustered included general revelation in nature (v. 24) and the writings of the Greeks' own poets (v. 28).

We will examine this account in detail in chapter 6. The point for now is that preaching gospel or law, without first applying apologetics, would have been ineffective with the Greek philosophers because they were pagans. They had no knowledge of Jesus Christ (v. 18) and certainly no interest in obeying Jewish law. Paul used apologetics to lay the groundwork for a presentation of the gospel in verses 30–31.

Modern Examples

Scenario One

Imagine that you are witnessing to someone who believes in God but has not accepted Jesus Christ as her personal Lord and Savior. She knows she's a sinner and that her lifestyle is unacceptable to God. She wants to change; she yearns to experience God's love and acceptance. What do we apply: law, gospel, or apologetics?

Gospel. Law and apologetics are unnecessary because this person neither holds the idea that she is good enough to warrant salvation independent of God's forgiveness through Jesus, nor does she harbor intellectual obstacles to faith or practice a non-Christian religion.

Generally, a person like this falls into one of two categories. The first recognizes that she's a sinner in need of God but believes that God will never forgive her horrible sins. Perhaps she has had an abortion or sold drugs to children. Whatever the reason, she's convinced she is doomed to hell, and there is nothing she can do about it.

The second doesn't know how to be saved. Her problem is not that she believes her sins are unforgivable, but that she doesn't know how to achieve forgiveness. She has never heard of or understood God's forgiveness through Christ. She doesn't know how to establish a relationship with Jesus whereby He becomes her personal Lord and Savior.

There are many people in liberal churches who fall into this latter category. In fact, I'm an example. As a child and teenager, when I went to church it was usually a liberal wing of the Presbyterian Church. I was even baptized (sprinkled) when I was twelve years old. But I don't remember ever hearing anything about receiving Jesus as my personal Lord and Savior (John 1:12). This did not occur until I attended an evangelical church as an adult.

In both of these cases—the one who thinks she can't be forgiven, as well as the one who doesn't know how to be saved—our evangelistic approach is to preach the good news of the gospel. These people need to see that they are forgiven for any and all sins. Jesus accepts them unconditionally where they are—regardless of their pasts. He saves them. He changes their lives from the inside out. They don't have to "clean up their act" before God accepts and forgives them.

Scenario Two

This person also believes in God. He knows who Jesus is and acknowledges that Jesus is the Son of God. He is somewhat familiar with other essential Christian doctrines and accepts them as well—or at least he doesn't disbelieve them. In other words, he identifies culturally with Christianity. He believes he is a Christian and, as a result, is saved.

However, this person has never made a personal commitment to Christ. Perhaps he was reared in a Christian home, went to Sunday school or Mass, and was taught to believe that the Bible is true. Consequently, he believes in Jesus but does not have a relationship with Him.

It's also possible that this person was discouraged—either by his parents, friends, or by the values of secular society—from ever going to church. In reality, it's not so much that he has rejected Christianity as that he knows little to nothing about it. Many of today's young people, raised in a post-Christian culture, have not received the benefit of even a rudimentary education in Christianity. Jesus is little more than a name seen on a billboard now and then.

In either case, this person assumes that he is saved because of the life he lives. He thinks a Christian is someone who is basically good in God's eyes. In other words, God will accept him in spite of his "little" sins. When questioned about this, he replies, "I don't drink, steal, or cheat on my spouse. I pay my taxes and give to charity. I even go to church now and then—and give to the offering. I'm a good person. I do the best I can. God will accept me into heaven."

You see, many people today think of sin and forgiveness in terms of moral relativity. They seem to believe their lives will be graded according to their behavior. If they've only committed little sins, such as telling white lies or stealing pens from the office, they figure they will receive high enough grades (A's and B's) to go to heaven. In-between sins, such as cheating on their taxes or adultery, can still be balanced by good deeds. So, although their lives may receive slightly lower grades (C's and D's), they still make it to heaven. Only really "bad" sins—drugs, rape, or murder, for example—receive the F that will send prople to hell.

What do we apply to the person who thinks he's good enough to get into heaven because of the life he lives—law, gospel, or apologetics?

Law. This person needs to see that becoming a Christian is a personal commitment to Jesus, not something into which one is born. Nor is salvation dependent on how good one is. This person needs to see that he is a sinner in need of a Savior. He can never be good enough to earn salvation on his own. Neither he, nor anyone else, can stand before God and claim he is worthy of heaven on his own merits.

Proclaiming law is a four-step process, and it's worth taking a moment to go over it step-by-step.

First, we point out from Scripture that everyone is a sinner. Everyone falls short of God's requirements for an obedient life, a life worthy of entry into heaven. No one can live a perfect, sin-free life (Rom. 3:10–18, 23).

Unbelievers need to understand that sin is not just bad deeds. In fact, people commit sins they are not even aware of, or realize are sins. For example, private, unexpressed thoughts can be sin (see Matt. 5:27–28). Not doing something when we know we should can also be a sin (see James 4:17).

Second, we explain that committing even one sin is equivalent to breaking all the law and causes one to fall under God's judgment (James 2:10). A holy God cannot tolerate sin. He would not be holy if He did.[4]

Third, the penalty of sin (breaking the law) is spiritual death, eternal separation from God (Rom. 6:23a).

Fourth, (the good news is) we can be forgiven for any and all sins through Jesus Christ (Rom. 6:23b).

Now, I'm not so presumptuous as to declare that all people who claim to be Christians but don't act like it are unsaved. There are carnal Christians (backslidden Christians living sinful lives, see 1 Cor. 3:15; 5:1–5; 2 Tim. 2:11–13). Moreover, as said, everyone sins, including Christians. But I am saying two things that "cultural Christians" need to hear.

First, I don't see how anyone can be certain of his salvation—*even if he is saved*—unless he has experienced the life-transforming power of God. If so-called cultural Christians are saved (and only God knows that for certain), we still need to encourage them to make Jesus the Lord of their lives, not just their Savior. They need to see, as Professor Philip Kenneson points out,

> It does absolutely no good for us to sit here and insist that the proposition "Jesus is Lord of the universe" is objectively true while at the same time we live our lives in such a way that this lordship remains completely invisible. If Christians feel compelled to claim that Jesus is Lord of the universe, then that lordship must be visible somewhere.[5]

Second, I'm certain that there are many thousands of people in this country today (including in the church) who are confident that they are destined for salvation when in fact they are not. They believe they are Christians when nothing in their lives demonstrates it. If someone were to ask them the question, "What is there about your life that would compel me to believe you are a Christian," they would have nothing to point to. Even if they claim to have made personal commitments to Jesus, they have never changed in terms of transformed lives since the day they first believed. They are more secular in their lifestyles than Christian. I believe that they're not saved.

Francis Schaeffer makes an observation here that's worth repeating:

> We should realize that the word *Christian* can legitimately be used in two ways. The primary meaning is: an individual who has come to God through the work of Christ. The second meaning must be kept distinct but also has validity. It is possible for an individual to live within the circle of that which a Christian consensus brings forth, even though he himself is not a Christian in the first sense.[6]

If I understand correctly what Schaeffer is saying here, he is pointing out that people can live within a Christian framework and promote Christian morals and ideals and yet not actually be Christians themselves. Certainly promoting Christian principles does not automatically make one a Christian.

Isn't this borne out in Scripture? In Matthew 7:21 Jesus says, "Not everyone who says to me, 'Lord, Lord,' will enter the kingdom of heaven, but only he who does the will of my Father who is in heaven."

I'm also reminded of the parable of the Pharisee and the tax collector in Luke 18:9–14. The Pharisee boasted of his good works and the money he gave to the temple. But the tax collector, who would not even look up to heaven, beat his breast and cried out, "God, have mercy on me, a sinner." Jesus concluded the parable by saying, "I tell you that this man, rather than the other, went home justified before God." People who are not justified before God do not go to heaven.

I firmly believe that these pseudo-Christians need to be evangelized every bit as much as the person who knows she's a miserable sinner. The odds are they aren't saved. They adhere, like the Pharisees, to a work-righteous concept of salvation, where one can *earn* entrance into heaven. One can be good enough to be saved independent of the work of Christ. Probably everyone has a family member, a friend, or knows someone who attends a church who fits this description.

I know it is not easy to do, but if we want to take evangelism seriously, we must confront these people. We do this through the avenue of proclaiming law. We point out the consequences of rejecting Jesus Christ and trying to gain heaven on our own terms. Jonathan Edwards, in his famous sermon "Sinners in the Hands of an Angry God," makes this relevant observation:

> If we could ask . . . [people in hell if] when they were alive and heard of hell, they ever expected to suffer its misery, they would doubtless say, "No, I never intended to come here. I had other plans. I thought I could manage well and my scheme was sound. I intended to carry out all of my plans, but death took me by surprise. I wasn't looking for it at that time or in that way. It came like a thief in the night. Death outsmarted me. God's wrath was too quick for me. O my cursed foolishness! All this time I was flattering

myself with empty dreams of what I would do later. And just when I was saying to myself, 'Peace and safety,' destruction overcame me."[7]

Scenario Three

This person rejects Christianity in its entirety. He does so for one of three reasons: (1) he practices some other religion, (2) he is an agnostic or an atheist, or (3) he harbors genuine intellectual objections that prevent him from seriously considering Christianity. Do we apply law, gospel, or apologetics?

Apologetics. Sharing the gospel with an agnostic, atheist, or a devout Buddhist will probably be a waste of time. At best, Jesus is acknowledged as merely a good person, a great prophet, or one of many gods; but He is not a member of the triune Godhead and Savior of the world in the Christian sense.

Likewise, proclaiming law to an agnostic, atheist, or Buddhist will probably be a waste of time. These people reject the Christian concept of God and the Bible as His revealed Word. Why then should they respond to what the Bible teaches in terms of sin and punishment? Apologetics is in order.

Here's how we apply apologetics in these cases. If the unbeliever is an agnostic or atheist, we provide compelling apologetic evidence that God exists and can be known. If an unbeliever encounters intellectual obstacles to Christianity, we identify these issues and overcome them. If the person adheres to a non-Christian religion, we challenge him to provide evidence for his belief. We point out inconsistencies, hidden assumptions, historical and prophetic inaccuracies, and lack of verification. We demonstrate that Christianity, alone among the world's religions, is internally and externally consistent, objectively verifiable, and subjectively true.[8]

Have I Left Out the Holy Spirit?

I fully realize that many agnostics, atheists, and followers of non-Christian religions have responded to the gospel without apologetics. This is because the Spirit of God prepared them to respond. Professor Mark Hanna correctly said,

> No apologetic can be truly Christian unless it conforms to Scriptural teaching about the Holy Spirit

> . . . Since the purpose of apologetics only termi-
> nates in a ministry to persons, it is radically defec-
> tive if it fails to accommodate itself to the work of
> the Holy Spirit in convicting and converting hu-
> man beings.
>
> Scripture is unequivocal in its teaching that
> apologetics, no less than the proclamation of the
> gospel, is ineffective without the action of the Holy
> Spirit upon the human heart (1 Cor. 12:3).[9]

The Holy Spirit is *always* the agent of conviction and conversion. However, it needs to be seen that the Holy Spirit can work through any avenue He chooses, including avenues other than the gospel. If God has not prepared a person to respond to gospel or law, apologetics comes into play. Indeed, apologetics is often used by the Holy Spirit to lay a foundation for future conversion. In other words, apologetics is planting and watering (pre-evangelism). This is a necessary first step on the road to salvation for many people (see 1 Cor. 3:6–7).

The Apologetic Mission

Let's tie this together. Law, gospel, and apologetics complement one another. They do not work independently; they work together. They are mutually inclusive.

We always initiate a witnessing opportunity with the gospel message (see chap. 2). If objections are raised, we switch to apologetics. When we have overcome an unbeliever's objections, we switch from apologetics back to gospel. However, if the person persists in rejecting the gospel in spite of the evidence, we apply law. We point out that she is an unsaved sinner and explain the consequences of willfully rejecting Jesus Christ. All three facets of evangelism work together.

One final thought before we move on. Even if we succeed in removing a person's intellectual objections to Christianity, or even if we have demonstrated the fallacious nature of his presently held religious or secular worldview, this alone may not be sufficient to compel an individual to accept Christianity.

Nevertheless, we have done something of great value. We have brought that person face-to-face with Jesus Christ. He is at a point where it is clear that his rejection of Christianity is not for intellectual reasons. Rather, it's willful and irrational. Why? Because the decision to reject Christianity in spite of the evidence is a *choice* one makes against the facts. And if it's willful and irrational, then the real reason for rejecting Christianity is a moral or emotional commitment to unbelief. The unbeliever does not want to accept the lifestyle changes that will naturally occur once Jesus is accepted as Lord and Savior, and once he begins to live a Christian life. He does not want to be accountable to God.

Sadly, an unbeliever who refuses to accept Christ for this reason does not realize that any lifestyle changes that occur are because God Himself places the desire to change (and the ability to do so) within him. This is the work of the Holy Spirit (see John 14:17; 1 Cor. 6:19; Gal. 5:24–25; 2 Tim. 1:7). Unbelievers do not have the indwelling Holy Spirit prior to conversion. They do not understand that it is the Holy Spirit who makes the changes, not themselves (1 Cor. 2:14). This needs to be explained.

Two Personality Types (ALSO!)

Besides the four kinds of people we encounter in terms of their blief in God and view of salvation, we can also group unbelievers into one of two personality types. This too is an aid to evangelism because it provides clues as to when apologetics is appropriate and when it should be avoided.

The first time I heard the idea of categorizing potential converts according to one of two personality types was in a taped seminar on apologetics taught by Dr. John Warwick Montgomery.[10] Dr. Montgomery referred to people as either "tough-minded" or "tender-minded." To some degree, this parallels modern psychology's concept of "right-brained" and "left-brained" personality types.

The idea is this. Once we judge that apologetics is the correct evangelistic approach, according to an unbeliever's view of God and salvation as outlined above, the tough- and tender-minded categories can be used to determine the kind of apologetics tactic we employ.

Let me give a brief summary of tough- and tender-minded personalities before we make an application.

Tough-Minded

Tough-minded people are primarily concerned with *objective* truth (truth that exists independent of personal beliefs, feelings, and experiences; truth that is verifiable). These people are rationally motivated; that is, things must be logical—make sense—before they'll believe it. They are the people who want so-called "scientific proof" before they will accept something. Hence, to the tough-minded, belief is bound up with evidence. Like Jack Webb in the 1960s television show *Dragnet*, they want "Just the facts, ma'am!"

Tough-minded people are the ones who usually raise intellectual objections to Christianity. The road to belief has many obstacles. They need their questions answered and their doubts resolved before they will accept biblical truth-claims. Consequently, tough-minded people are not moved by subjective religious experiences. Personal testimonies or dramatic, life-transforming conversion experiences are usually unconvincing to them.

Tough-minded people tend to look for natural explanations for religious phenomena. They are skeptics of anything with a hint of the supernatural. For example, a religious conversion is merely a psychological phenomenon. A miraculous healing is attributed to the so-called power of suggestion or to positive thinking. Answered prayer is seen as coincidence, a natural occurrence whose timing simply coincided with prayer; it would have happened anyway.

Although we should initiate a witnessing encounter with the gospel, in most cases this approach is ineffective with tough-minded people. They almost always raise objections or shrug us off. We usually have to work our way up to a gospel presentation by removing intellectual obstacles. In a sense, we have to earn the right to give a gospel presentation.

On the brighter side, as Montgomery explains, tough-minded people are more likely to listen to the facts and go with them. If they are convinced by the evidence, they are more likely to alter their existing worldview assumptions and go with Christianity.

As with all genuine conversions to Christianity, the Holy Spirit is involved in the conversion of tough-minded people. But tough-minded people come to Christ through their heads rather than their hearts, through their intellects rather than their feelings. In other words, rather than law or gospel, the Holy Spirit uses the intellect—often through extra-biblical (apologetic) evidences—to reveal spiritual truth to tough-minded people. Apologetics is the key to evangelizing these individuals.

As an interesting side note, once a tough-minded person becomes converted, he finds great pleasure in continuing to pursue the intellectual side of Christianity. A theological study can be as spiritually uplifting to him as a praise song is to the tender-minded. Speaking of himself, C. S. Lewis said,

> I tend to find the doctrinal books often more helpful in devotion than the devotional books, and I rather suspect that the same experience may await many others. I believe that many who find that "nothing happens" when they sit down, or kneel down, to a book of devotion, would find that the heart sings unbidden while they are working their way through a tough bit of theology with a pipe in their teeth and a pencil in their hand.[11]

Tender-Minded

Tender-minded people, on the other hand, are more influenced by *subjective* truth (truth that is not based on anything outside one's personal thoughts, feelings, and experiences; truth that is not dependent on external verification). Tender-minded people are sensitive to feelings. They crave emotional fulfillment more than intellectual fulfillment. Does Christianity "feel" right? Does it satisfy my deepest emotional and spiritual needs? Will it heal my hurts and bring me inner happiness and peace of mind?

Normally, tender-minded people do not need extra-biblical evidences to convince them that Christian truth-claims are valid. It doesn't matter whether Christianity is verified by historical, scientific, legal, and other proofs. Subjective proof—inner confirmation—is enough. What matters is that Christianity provides a heartfelt relationship with God and that it explains the world in a way that is emotionally and spiritually satisfying.

Tender-minded people are usually responsive to real-life

accounts of the life-changing power of God. They will willingly listen to our personal testimonies and other religious experiences. How has faith in Christ changed *our* lives? What does a relationship with Jesus mean to *us*? With them we share the emotional healing and inner strength that a relationship with Jesus provides. In other words, we demonstrate though our own experiences how Christianity appeals to the hearts and souls of people.

Tender-minded people are also sensitive to word pictures, stories, and analogies. We can use these as subjective apologetic tools. Alister McGrath gives examples of this that are worth quoting. Although his focus is explaining theological concepts through analogy, I believe his illustrations apply equally well to tender-minded people.

> Theology is able to use words in such a way as to offer some pointers for the benefit of those who have yet to discover what it feels like to experience God. It uses a cluster of key words to try and explain what it is like to know God, by analogy with words associated with human experience. It is like forgiveness—in other words, if you can imagine what it feels like to be forgiven for a really serious offense, you can begin to understand the Christian experience of forgiveness. It is like reconciliation— if you can imagine the joy of being reconciled to someone who matters very much to you, you can get a glimpse of what the Christian experience of coming home to God is like. It is like coming home after being away and alone for a long time, and perhaps fully expecting never to be able to return. Apologetics uses analogies like these to try and signpost . . . the Christian experience of God, for the benefit of those who [like the tender-minded] have yet to have this transforming experience.[12]

In light of the needs of these two distinct personality types, it is beneficial to determine whether the person you are witnessing to is tough- or tender-minded and to tailor your approach accordingly. A tough-minded person needs hard evidence. A tender-minded person needs to see that Christianity works, that it will meet personal needs at an emotional and spiritual level, and that it's personally satisfying.

Summary

By knowing what kind of an unbeliever you are encountering in terms of belief in God and perception of salvation; by knowing when to apply law, gospel, or apologetics; and by discerning the difference between a tough-minded and tender-minded person, your effectiveness in evangelism will be greatly enhanced.

Presenting law or applying apologetics to a tender-minded person who already knows she's a sinner separated from God, is unnecessary. She doesn't need convincing. Share what Jesus has done for you and will do for her. Apply gospel.

The tough- or tender-minded person who thinks he's "good enough" to enter heaven on his own merits needs to see that no one is sinless, no one is to stand before a just and holy God and plead innocent. No one gains admittance to heaven based on his own behavior. No one's *that* good. Apply law.

For the tough-minded person adhering to a non-Christian religion, explain that her existing beliefs, no matter what they are, will not stand up to critical scrutiny. Demonstrate that Christianity is the only sustainable option in the area of religious truth. Apply apologetics.

For the tender-minded person adhering to a non-Christian religion, illustrate from your own experiences how Christianity provides true emotional and spiritual fulfillment. Explain that other religions are *demonstrably* counterfeit. Therefore, any emotional or spiritual fulfillment one experiences through them is likewise counterfeit. Apply apologetics graced with gospel.

Giving your personal testimony to a tough-minded agnostic or atheist, who considers all religions human fabrications, is likely to be ineffective. Identify and respond to his particular issues. Apply apologetics.

On the other hand, giving your personal testimony or sharing your religious experiences with a tender-minded atheist or agnostic may be effective. Objective apologetic evidence may not be as important as subjective confirmation.

The apologetic mission, then, in all these cases, is to demonstrate that if God exists at all, and if He has revealed Himself to humanity, it is only through the Christian religion. There are no alternatives. Tailoring our evangelism according to the needs of the individual to whom we are witnessing will help us reach this goal. I believe this is what the apostle Paul meant when he wrote, concerning his own witnessing approach, "I have become all things to all men so that by all possible means I might save some" (1 Cor. 9:22).

Endnotes

1. Peter Kreeft and Ronald K. Tacelli, *Handbook of Christian Apologetics* (Downers Grove, Ill.: InterVarsity, 1994), 202.
2. Ibid., 203
3. Stephen Neill, *Christian Faiths and Other Faiths* (Downers Grove, Ill.: InterVarsity, 1984), 189.
4. This doesn't mean that all sins are equal. In Matthew 23:23 Jesus points out that there are "more important matters of the law." In John 19:11, He states that Caiaphas "is guilty of a greater sin" than Pilate. And in Luke 12:47–48, Jesus tells a parable in which a person who does not know he is sinning receives less punishment than the one who does. These three passages imply that some sins are worse than others, and that the punishment will fit the sin. The point is, all sins are intolerable to God, and were it not for Jesus, we would receive just punishment for even one sin.
5. Philip D. Kenneson, "There's No Such Thing As Objective Truth, and It's a Good Thing, Too," in *Christian Apologetics in the Postmodern World*, ed. Timothy R. Phillips and Dennis L. Okholm (Downers Grove, Ill.: InterVarsity, 1995), 168.
6. Francis A. Schaeffer, *How Should We Then Live?* (Old Tappan, N.J.: Revell, 1976), 110.
7. Jonathan Edwards, "Sinners in the Hands of an Angry God," in *Made Easier to Read*, ed. John Jeffery Fanella (Phillipsburg, N.J.: R & R Publishing, 1996), 14.
8. What I mean by "subjectively true" is that Christianity works. It alone provides answers to profound and perplexing questions in a way that is in complete harmony with human nature as most people understand it and live it out. For example, only Christianity

adequately explains the source of evil and the solution to human suffering (see my book *Defending Your Faith* [Grand Rapids: Kregel, 1997], chap. 13). Only Christianity adequately accounts for the undeniable existence of human sin. Only Christianity is transcultural in that its moral teachings intuitively fit all cultures and all periods of history.

9. Mark M. Hanna, *Crucial Questions in Apologetics* (Grand Rapids: Baker, 1981), 60–61.

10. John Warwick Montgomery, "A Word for Those Who Think with Their Feelings." This is a portion of a taped seminar titled *Sensible Christianity*, recorded by the Institute for Law and Theology, Newport Beach, Calif., 1981.

11. C. S. Lewis, *God in the Dock* (Grand Rapids: Eerdmans, 1970), 205.

12. Alister McGrath, *A Passion for Truth* (Downers Grove, Ill.: InterVarsity, 1996), 86–87.

2

The Ten Commandments of Apologetics

Possessing answers to the tough questions and refuting non-Christian religious and secular worldviews do not automatically result in a victory for Christ. Equally important to possessing knowledge of apologetics is the ability to apply it effectively; that is, the ability to engage unbelievers in a way that they will listen, understand, and consider.

This chapter contains the "do's" and "don'ts" of apologetics.[1] On the "do" side are the principles of sound apologetics tactics. On the "don't" side are the pitfalls of poor apologetics—things to avoid. Together they provide the ground rules for effective apologetics evangelism. You will see these principles applied frequently throughout the remainder of this book.

Gospel First, Apologetics Second

Although apologetics is a valuable tool in evangelism—a vital tool at times—the gospel of Christ is what people must ultimately hear in order to be saved (Rom. 1:16). It is wrong to assume that every unbeliever harbors intellectual objections to Christianity. Hence not every evangelistic situation will require an apologetics defense.

Always try to start a witnessing encounter with the gospel. If the unbeliever responds to the gospel, forget apologetics and pursue proclamation—continue to proclaim the "good news" of Christ.

Sometimes it's not possible to start with the gospel. In many encounters with unbelievers, you'll find yourself responding to challenges or answering questions concerning issues far removed from the gospel, and the plan of salvation will have to come later. "Why is there so much suffering if God is so good?" "Why do you Christians condemn to hell people who've never even heard of Jesus Christ?" "You don't take the Bible literally, do you?" And so on.

The job of apologetics is to pave the way for a presentation of the gospel. In this sense, apologetics is "pre-evangelism." It identifies and removes intellectual obstacles that hinder someone from considering the gospel message.

Stay with the Essentials

Most non-Christians know little about the Bible or what Christians believe, and what they think they know is often in error. In his book *God in the Dock*, C. S. Lewis describes the formation of the Socratic Club at Oxford in the early 1940s. The club met weekly to debate with skeptics the pros and cons of Christianity. Lewis recounts that

> We of the Christian party discovered that the weight of the skeptical attack did not always come where we expected it; our opponents had to correct what seems to us their *almost bottomless ignorance of the Faith they supposed themselves to be rejecting.* (emphasis mine)[2]

Then as now, even scholarly skeptics are woefully ignorant of much of Christianity.

When sharing the gospel, avoid theological subjects that will be confusing to unbelievers, like eschatology or predestination. Likewise, avoid controversial, in-house issues such as speaking in tongues or wine drinking. We should never muddy the waters of good evangelism with topics Christians may rightfully disagree on (see Rom. 14 and 1 Cor. 8).

In short, stay with the *essentials*—areas of doctrine that unite Christians, not divide them. The apostle Paul summarizes the essentials in 1 Corinthians 15:3–4: "For I deliver to you as of first importance what I also received, that Christ died for our sins according to the Scriptures, and that he was buried, and that he was raised on the third day according to the Scriptures." This passage encapsulates the essential Christian message, the "Good News" of the gospel: the death and resurrection of our Lord Jesus Christ for the forgiveness of sins (see Rom. 5:8; 6:23).[3]

Don't be discouraged when an unbeliever fails to respond to the gospel. The Holy Spirit is the agent of conviction, not us. In John 6:44 Jesus says, "No one can come to me, unless the Father who sent him draws him" (see also Acts 11:19–21; 16:14; 1 Cor. 3:6–7). Take the pressure off yourself. No matter how much we wish a loved one to be saved, we can't save him or her ourselves, and we should not feel guilty because our words seem ineffective. Keep that person in prayer. As James said, "The prayer of a righteous man is powerful and effective" (5:16).

Law, gospel, and apologetics are tools of the Holy Spirit. All can create an environment in which the Holy Spirit is free to work. But it is always the Holy Spirit who convicts, convinces, and converts. The "Four Spiritual Laws," the "Roman Road to Salvation," your personal testimony, or the most eloquent and compelling sermon will not save anyone unless God intends it at that moment.

So, as much as possible, always begin a witnessing encounter with the gospel. Confirm the message by sharing your personal testimony. This will make the gospel message subjectively real by demonstrating the life-transforming power of the Holy Spirit in your own life. If God has not prepared that person to respond to the gospel, he or she will raise an objection. When this happens, switch from proclamation to apologetics.

Remember Your Goal

Christian apologetics can be an instrument of God for ushering unbelievers into the kingdom. The goal of apologetics (its purpose as an instrument of God) is to overcome intellectual obstacles to Christianity so that unbelievers are willing to consider the gospel.

This does not necessarily mean that we must give an unbeliever all possible solutions to his objections or even our personal choice of answers. But it does mean that we give *reasonable* and *biblically sustainable* solutions. We provide intelligent responses to demonstrate that what unbelievers think are insurmountable obstacles to Christianity have rational and justifiable explanations.

What do I mean when I say we don't have to give all possible solutions to perceived problems or even our personal choice of answers? Let me explain.

Apologetics is not theology. As John Warwick Montgomery points out, there is more latitude in apologetics than in theology. We don't have to give the definitive theological answer to any issue, only an appropriate answer that can be defended scripturally. This concept is important enough to warrant two examples. The first I borrow from Dr. Montgomery.

Evolution

For many unbelievers, evolution is an obstacle to faith. They assume that evolution disproves creation, thus demonstrating that the Bible is in error. But evolution doesn't have to be an obstacle to Christianity. One can believe in evolution and still receive Jesus Christ as Lord and Savior. Romans 10:9 says, "If you confess with your mouth, 'Jesus is Lord,' and believe in your heart that God raised him from the dead, you will be saved." It *doesn't* say, "If you confess with your mouth, 'Jesus is Lord,' and believe in your heart that God raised him from the dead, *and also believe in seven-day creation,* you will be saved."

Obviously, if one rejects creation in favor of *naturalistic* evolution, one is an atheist. Nevertheless, we don't have to convince an unbeliever that it's seven-day creation or nothing, that if "you don't renounce evolution entirely you can't be a Christian!" Instead, we point out that *theistic evolution* (the belief that evolution is true but that God initiated it) is acceptable to many Christians and need not interfere with someone receiving Jesus Christ as Lord and Savior. In fact, we continue, there are many scholarly, evangelical Christians who love the Lord and who believe in the authority of Scriptures but who hold to theistic evolution. This alone proves that evolution does not have to be an obstacle to Christianity. Otherwise, these people would not be Christians.

Now, we may not personally agree with this position (and, as Montgomery suggests, we should say so), but it does represent a rational argument that can be sustained on biblical grounds—

assuming one views the creation account as a poetic narrative rather than a historical description. In this way we can avoid an unnecessary discussion on creation versus evolution and move on to "Who is Jesus Christ?"—the goal of all apologetics.

Now, it may be that the unbeliever will want to push this issue anyway. If he insists that any kind of evolution disproves the existence of God, we must respond. This means providing apologetic evidence for creation.[4]

Fate of the Heathen

Here's a second example where it's usually wise to avoid a theological discussion. Many unbelievers struggle over the fate of those who never had the opportunity to hear the gospel message—the so-called innocent savages. They believe Christianity teaches that these people are automatically doomed to hell.

Some theologians argue from Scripture that these people are not the "elect" and therefore are destined for hell. Other theologians (and I believe the majority) argue from Scripture that God will judge people according to the information they have received about Him (see Rom. 1:18–20; 2:13–16) and what they do with it (see John 15:22–25; 1 Tim. 1:13).

The problem is, whether true or not, the former view is the one most unbelievers assume that all Christians believe. Hence, they use it as an argument against Christianity.

Now ask yourself: Which is the softer apologetic response—the one that claims the heathen are automatically condemned to hell or the one that claims they are judged according to the information they receive and how they respond to it?

You see, a definitive answer to the fate of the heathen is a theological issue, not an apologetics issue. We need to keep our apologetics simple and avoid theological speculation. Rather than get involved in a theological debate over this issue, it is better to point out that the Bible teaches that salvation is available to everyone through Jesus Christ (1 John 2:2). And although we don't know for certain the fate of people who never personally hear of Jesus, we do know for certain that God is just and loving and does not want anyone to perish (1 Tim. 2:4; 2 Peter 3:9). People go to hell because they choose to reject God's offered hand of salvation—not because of what they don't know.

Again, as with theistic evolution, you may not personally agree with this position, but it is an approach that assures unbelievers that the heathen will be treated fairly.

We must be careful, however, that unbelievers don't interpret this to mean that everyone is saved. Unbelievers need to know that people who have the opportunity to know and receive Jesus but reject Him are damned, which, of course, would include the person you are talking to at the moment! (see Deut. 24:16; Isa. 59:2).

The Challenge

The ultimate goal of apologetics is to bring unbelievers to the point where they must admit, even if only to themselves, that if they reject Jesus Christ, they are *not* doing so for intellectual reasons. People can make moral or emotional (and irrational) commitments to unbelief, but they can't legitimately reject Christianity on intellectual grounds.

This is worth restating. Apologetics confronts unbelievers head-on and forces them to recognize the real reasons they spurn Christianity. By overcoming intellectual objections, apologetics removes excuses and rationalizations. It compels unbelievers to admit that they don't want to be Christian because they don't want to give up their "playboy" lifestyles or their shady business practices or their comfortable and self-serving religious worldviews; or perhaps they will come to understand that they simply don't want to submit to God. But whatever the reason, it's not because Christianity is untrue, inconsistent, or unable to justify its truth-claims.

Never Give People a Problem

We should never force apologetics on someone or create illegitimate reasons to use it. Studying apologetics can be so affirming to one's faith that it frequently leads to a new zeal for evangelism. I hope it does for you. The impulse is to go out and confront everyone you know and challenge their misbeliefs (especially people who may have tripped you up in the past).

However, remember rule number one: "gospel first, apologetics second." Apologetics is a tool for evangelism, not an excuse to argue. It's a means to an end (the gospel)—not the end itself. It would be foolish, for example, to corner an unbeliever and make a statement like, "I bet you reject Christianity because you've heard the Bible contains contradictions" and then start hammering her with arguments supporting the reliability and accuracy of Scripture.

Her problem may not be related to the Bible at all. Perhaps the death of a loved one has caused her to reject God. In this case, even apologetics is not appropriate. Christian love and understanding may be all she needs. Or perhaps she's convinced that all Christians are intolerant and narrow-minded. In this case, your attack will only strengthen her unbelief—not remove it!

Again, the rule here is, whenever possible, give the gospel first. Let the unbeliever raise objections. Apologetics is a tool for evangelism, not for winning arguments.

Find out the Real Problem

Sometimes unbelievers will raise issues against Christianity that do not mirror their real concerns. It may be that they feel more comfortable discussing a popular argument, such as alleged contradictions in Scripture, rather than what's really bothering them. Or perhaps the real issue is not related to apologetics at all. A bad experience in church has turned many people away from Christianity.

Whatever the issues, Christian apologists must identify them and respond accordingly. Sometimes we may have to deal with peripheral concerns or non-apologetics matters before we can discover the real obstacle to faith.

Objections to Christianity fall into one of three categories: emotional, willful, or intellectual. Emotion issues, such as anger at God or a bad experience with church or an individual Christian, are not solved through apologetics. People with these problems need to have personal friendships with mature, committed Christians. They need to experience Christian love and observe Christian faith in action.

What about people who willfully reject Christianity in spite of our best efforts at proclaiming gospel, law, or apologetics? These people have made a commitment to unbelief. Their minds are made up and they don't want to be bothered with the facts. Normally, the best we can do in these cases is to pray that God will open their hearts and minds to truth and provide us with opportunities to share.

Finally, to the people with intellectual obstacles, we apply apologetics. If we fail to identify their real issues and respond only to the peripheral ones or apply the wrong approach (such as sharing the gospel with someone who needs apologetics—see chap. 1), we will never convince unbelievers that Christianity is true. It's crucial that we identify whatever the obstacle is that stands between an unbeliever and faith in Jesus Christ.

Avoid Distractions

Lifestyle

Unless unbelievers make it an issue themselves, don't get distracted by their lifestyles. Apologetics deals with intellectual obstacles, not moral issues. That a man and woman are living together out of wedlock should not prevent us from sharing Jesus Christ as Lord and Savior. Nor should we let it interfere with a discussion of apologetics.

I was discussing this particular point in class when one of my students raised her hand and said, "I have a relative who is a homosexual. Every time I witness to him, we eventually come to this issue, and I just can't get beyond it. What do I do?"

The answer is to go around it. God will deal with moral issues once a person sees his or her need to become a Christian. It is the Holy Spirit who convicts people of sin (John 16:8). He will show unbelievers those areas in their lives that need to be changed—and then empower them to make the necessary changes—once He calls them into the family of Christ.

Sanctification is a process that begins *after* we're saved—it's not a requirement before we're saved. A past life of sin is not an obstacle to faith, but our condemnation and our threats of divine punishment can be. Jesus came to heal the sick (sinners) not the healthy (Mark 2:17). We would not need Christ if we weren't sinners.

Peripheral Issues

The second distraction to avoid is peripheral issues—issues that are not apologetic in nature or do not further the cause of evangelism. Some unbelievers like to argue just for the sake of arguing and are unwilling to examine critically the decisive issues: Who is Jesus Christ? Is salvation only through Him? Is the Bible true?

These people characteristically interrupt, change the subject, or wander off on rabbit trails.

A favorite tactic of these unbelievers is to argue over some inane matter that has nothing to do with whether Christianity is true or not, such as the death penalty. Christians involved in cult evangelism frequently encounter this ploy. In order to avoid discussing relevant issues, many cultists prefer to argue over soul sleep, blood atonement, or some other irrelevant dogma.

How do we respond to these individuals? By controlling the conversation. Keep them on track by constantly returning to the issue at hand. Try to move the conversation to "Who is Jesus Christ?" Point out that you are willing to listen to them, but they in turn must give you the same respectful attention, or there is no use continuing the discussion. Insist that they let you respond to one issue before they raise another one. Again, control the conversation.

Apply Evangelistic and Missionary Techniques

This means two things. First, as said before, the ultimate goal of apologetics is evangelistic. The purpose is to bring people as quickly and as efficiently as possible to the point where they renounce their non-Christian worldviews and accept Jesus Christ as Lord and Savior. In this sense, apologetics is "pre-evangelism."

Second, like all missionary work, apologetics involves seeking unbelievers on their own turf. In Romans 10:14–15 Paul writes:

> How can they hear without someone preaching to them? And how can they preach unless they are sent? As it is written, "How beautiful are the feet of those who bring good news!"

And in 15:20–21 he adds:

> It has always been my ambition to preach the gospel where Christ was not known, so that I would not be building on someone else's foundation. Rather, as it is written: "Those who were not told about him will see, and those who have not heard will understand."

Paul reminds us in these two passages that (1) unbelievers must hear and receive the gospel before they can be saved, and (2) Christian evangelists (and apologists) should seek "new territory."

It's up to Christians to bring unbelievers saving knowledge of Jesus Christ, wherever they are. Paul set the example. He sought Jews in the synagogues and Gentiles in the marketplaces. He argued with the Greek philosophers before the Areopagus in pagan Athens (Acts 17). Indeed, Paul traveled much of the known world in his quest to share our Lord Jesus Christ.

In 1 Corinthians 9:19–22, Paul provides guidelines on how an evangelist/missionary/apologist interacts with unbelievers in order to get a fair hearing for the gospel. He states:

> Though I am free and belong to no man, I make myself a slave to everyone, to win as many as possible. To the Jews I became like a Jew, to win the Jews. To those under the law I became like one under the law (though I myself am not under the law), so as to win those under the law. To those not having the law [Gentiles] I became like one not having the law (though I am not free from God's law but am under Christ's law), so as to win those not having the law. To the weak I became weak, to win the weak. I have become all things to all men so that by all possible means I might save some.

In Acts 16:1–3 Paul puts this teaching into practice. In this instance, Paul circumcised Timothy so that he would be accepted among the Jews even though Timothy was not obligated to be circumcised (also see Acts 21:17–26). Paul was willing to conform to Jewish ritual in order to witness to the Jews, as long as it didn't compromise the gospel or violate biblical principles.

By whatever means necessary, Paul endeavored to make the gospel relevant and applicable to unbelievers regardless of their existing beliefs and customs.

Likewise, we too can be apologetic missionaries. Our neighborhoods, workplaces, and social clubs are fertile missionary fields. We can invite unbelievers to church, home Bible studies, and into our homes. Like Paul, we can leave our comfort zone and seek unbelievers in "new territory." This may include door-to-door or street-corner evangelism, college classrooms, New Age fairs, and "open forum" Bible studies designed specifically for unbelievers.

Our goal in all cases is to present the Christian worldview by responding to misconceptions about Christianity, by answering questions, and by demonstrating the relevance of Christianity in a post-Christian world. As the late Francis Schaeffer said: "Apologetics should not be merely an academic subject, a new kind of scholasticism. It should be thought out and practiced in the rough and tumble of living contact with the present generation."[5] To sum up, using apologetics as a species of evangelism and missionary work means seeking opportunities to share the gospel and to defend our faith as Paul says, "in season and out of season" (2 Tim. 4:2).

Know What You Believe (Defensive Apologetics)

The Lord has charged us with the responsibility to evangelize the lost (Acts 1:8) and to defend our faith (1 Peter 3:15; Jude 3). In order to do this, we must be able to do three things:

- First, we must understand and be able to explain orthodox biblical doctrines, especially the essentials of our faith.
- Second, we must be able to demonstrate these doctrines from Scripture and back up what we believe in the Bible. This requires systematically studying the Bible.
- Third, we must be able to defend Christian truth-claims and present rational and verifiable apologetics evidence whenever necessary.

This is defensive apologetics. It entails being prepared to answer the challenges and objections unbelievers raise.

Know What Unbelievers Believe (Offensive Apologetics)

Whereas defensive apologetics is defending Christianity, offensive apologetics is challenging the unbelievers' beliefs. In a later chapter we'll see how this is done. For now, it needs to be seen that offensive apologetics requires an understanding of what un-believers believe.

Before a missionary goes into a foreign culture he learns as much as he can about that culture: the religious beliefs, the language, social customs, ethical behavior, religious and cultural taboos, and so on. Such insights allow a missionary to discern how best to initiate an evangelistic strategy.

In a similar fashion, Christian apologists must learn what un-believers believe. This is especially necessary for apologists wit-nessing to people of non-Christian religions and Christian cults. It's impossible to formulate an offensive apologetics unless we understand what these religions teach.

The lesson here is *be prepared*. Do your homework. Learn what you can about the religions and the secular worldviews you are likely to encounter at home, work, school, and play.

Don't Be Intimidated

Most non-Christians have little knowledge of the Bible, and few have read even a portion of it. They seldom ask sophisticated questions or need in-depth answers. In fact, it's best to keep our responses as simple and specific as possible.

In many cases, unbelievers are so ignorant of Christianity that they have a hard time even articulating their arguments, let alone offering any evidence for their beliefs. For example, when a non-Christian claims that the Bible is "full of contradictions," he is seldom able, when asked, to point to one such contradiction. He probably never studied the Bible and got his opinions from hear-say: "Everyone knows. . . ."

This is not to say that there are no astute non-Christians with sophisticated arguments. But most of the people Christians encounter are friends, relatives, coworkers, fellow students, and neighbors. Their criticisms are usually the product of anti-Christian sentiments absorbed from the media, TV and movies, secular colleges and high schools, and so on. Seldom are their criticisms well-thought-out arguments.

If you do encounter questions you can't answer, or arguments you can't refute, admit it. Our response to all challenges must be honest. However, not having a response at the moment is not the same as saying that there is no response. Point this out. Assure the unbeliever that there is an answer to his question or argument and that you will find it. This provides an opportunity to meet again.

If you won't be seeing that person again, research the problem anyway. Next time you'll have a response if the issue arises.

Keep the Right Attitude

Several years ago two young Mormon missionaries knocked on my door, and I invited them in. The discussion did not go well for them, and they asked if they could return with their "superior." I agreed, and the four of us met about a week later. As the three were leaving the second time, one of them turned to me and said, "You know, you're the nicest person we've ever talked to!"

People who know me well chuckle when they hear this story. I have a reputation for possessing, to use John Trent's animal analogy, a "lion" personality. My point is, that flattering comment did not accurately reflect my normal behavior when discussing, say, debatable issues with Christian friends. I was being polite and respectful as any Christian should be when sharing with unbelievers. That's how we're supposed to behave.

But their comment brings to mind how rude and self-righteous Christians can be. One can only imagine how many stories cult evangelists can tell about unfriendly, even belligerent, Christians. Part of the reason for this, as I believe the late Dr. Walter Martin aptly put it, is that the average Christian can be tied up like a pretzel in about five minutes by the average cultist. When this happens, it's not surprising that Christians become frustrated, angry, and full of hostility.

The lesson here is that being discourteous or rude does not create an environment that encourages the work of the Holy Spirit. I could have gotten angry and argumentative with the Mormon missionaries, but that would have only reinforced their conviction that Christianity is in error. When people get rude and defensive with us, don't we assume it's because they know they're wrong and can't admit it?

The primary apologetics text in Scripture is 1 Peter 3:15: "Sanctify Christ as Lord in your hearts, always being ready to make a defense [Greek: *apologia*] to everyone who asks you to give an account for the hope that is in you, *yet with gentleness and reverence*" (emphasis mine).

Apologetics is giving a reasoned defense of Christian truth-claims, in particular of the authenticity of the Bible and the deity and resurrection of Jesus Christ. But a "reasoned defense" never includes quarreling. In religious discussions, arguing usually results in a win/lose situation: we may win the argument but lose a conversion. So we want to avoid being hostile, quarrelsome, or confrontational. As Paul instructs, apologetics should be done with "gentleness and reverence."

Critical thinking and persuasive reasoning are tools of the trade in apologetics. And for a trained apologist, it's not difficult to thwart arguments against the gospel. Unfortunately, this does not automatically result in a conversion. Evangelist Jim Petersen makes an insightful comment here.

> Why does a person . . . make a decision to become a Christian at all? He may make a decision simply because he has run out of arguments against the gospel. He can no longer come up with any good reason why he shouldn't become a Christian—even though he really doesn't want to. It's usually not very difficult to destroy a person's arguments against the gospel. Often when someone finds himself in this position, he simply says, "You win." He gives in to the truth, but he doesn't submit his life to Christ. His will remains intact.[6]

Christians have religious truth and the evidence to prove it. The problem is, no one likes to lose an argument. So good apologetics convinces without being offensive.

How do we "argue" so as not to make people lose face? The apostle Paul gives us the answer:

> Be wise in the way you act toward outsiders; make the most of every opportunity. Let your conversation be always full of grace, seasoned with salt, so that you may know how to answer everyone. (Col. 4:5–6)

> And the Lord's servant must not quarrel; instead,
> he must be kind to everyone, able to teach, not
> resentful. Those who oppose him he must gently
> instruct, in the hope that God will grant them
> repentance leading them to a knowledge of the
> truth. . . . (2 Tim. 2:24–25)

By following this advice, Christian apologists will seem not only interested in sharing truth, but genuinely interested in the unbeliever as a person. This is the surest way to earn the right to share the gospel.

Endnotes

1. Again, I am indebted in this chapter to a taped seminar by my former professor, Dr. John Warwick Montgomery, titled *Sensible Christianity*, produced by the Institute for Law and Theology, Newport Beach, Calif., 1981. In the tape titled, "The Do's and Don'ts of Apologetics," Dr. Montgomery suggests seven "ground rules" for apologetics. I have borrowed several of his headings and their contents (and created some of my own), and I have tried to be faithful to his suggestions.
2. C. S. Lewis, *God in the Dock* (Grand Rapids: Eerdmans, 1970), 127.
3. A good summary of essential Christian doctrine is found in the Nicene and Athanasian Creeds. They are statements of faith accepted not only by Protestants but also by Roman Catholics and the Eastern Orthodox.
4. Dan Story, *Defending Your Faith* (Grand Rapids: Kregel, 1997), chap. 11.
5. Francis A. Schaeffer, *The God Who Is There* (Downers Grove, Ill.: InterVarsity, 1968), 140.
6. Jim Petersen, *Evangelism As a Lifestyle* (Colorado Springs: NavPress, 1984), 118.

3

The Foundational Issue

Defending the Bible

I gave a copy of my book *Defending Your Faith* to a friend I've known since high school. We got together after he'd read the book, and I asked him what he thought of it.

"I have to admit," he said, "it's not very convincing."

"Why?" I asked. "What do you mean?"

"Because everything in the book seems to depend on whether or not the Bible is true."

I was surprised at his response. "That's *very* perceptive of you," I replied, "because that's exactly the case!"

You see, my friend was perceptive enough to recognize that the very survival of Christianity depends on the reliability and authority of the Bible. Without realizing it, he had identified the fundamental apologetic issue to which Christians must attend: Is the Bible reliable? This, above all other matters, must be substantiated.

Why is this? Because Christianity stands or falls on the merits of scriptural veracity. All Christian truth-claims, including the deity and resurrection of Jesus Christ, depend on the truthfulness of Holy Scripture.

Where do we learn precise information about the nature of God? The Bible. Where do we meet Jesus and learn what He has done for us? The Bible. Where do we learn how to be saved, how to grow spiritually, and how to become filled with the Holy Spirit? The Bible.

If the Bible is reliable—if it tells the truth—it's authoritative. To put this another way, since the Bible claims to be God's Word (2 Tim. 3:16), if it's true, it's authoritative. And if the Bible is God's Word (authoritative), then what it says about Jesus, salvation, miracles, heaven, hell, answered prayer, and all other matters relevant to our faith is true. On the other hand, if the Bible is not reliable—or if apologists can't demonstrate its reliability— unbelievers are justified in raising intellectual objections and harboring doubts concerning its spiritual claims. It's the proven reliability (and hence the authority) of the Bible that elevates Christianity above all other religions.

How Do We Know the Bible Is Reliable?

At this point it's necessary to qualify what apologists mean when they claim they can prove the reliability and authenticity of the Bible. Obviously vast portions of Scripture, standing alone, are not provable: the existence of heaven and hell, the indwelling of the Holy Spirit, the existence of angels and demons, the virgin birth, and salvation through Christ are a few examples. These *spiritual* truth-claims are impossible to check out and to verify empirically.

However, it's not necessary to prove any of these truths in order to establish the reliability and authority of Scripture. Let me explain.

Christian apologists can demonstrate that the Bible is truthful and reliable in every area in which it is possible to investigate: its historical, archeological, cultural, scientific, and geographical claims; its textual coherence and the accuracy of its transmission down through the ages; the precision with which its many hundreds of prophecies have been fulfilled; its accuracy in explaining human nature as we experience it; and its ability to meet people's deepest emotional needs.

If the Bible stands the test of critical scrutiny in these areas, Christians are justified—we are being logically consistent—in concluding that the Bible is equally truthful and reliable in the spiritual (non-testable) arena as well. How do we know that angels exist and that salvation is through Jesus Christ alone? Because they are revealed in a book of proven accuracy and reliability.[1] In other words, we can demonstrate that the Bible is divine revelation to the highest level of certainty attainable in the area of religious truth, to a probability far beyond any reasonable doubt.[2]

How does this compare with other religious holy books? The fact is, no other religious book in existence meets these criteria. Indeed, all religious writings except the Bible are conspicuous in their lack of verification. The Bible, alone among the world's holy books, is God's written disclosure of spiritual and moral truth.

Inevitably, upon investigation and in spite of their claims, all other religious writings and philosophies can be demonstrated to have arisen from one or a combination of the following.

1. The words and writings of false prophets who claim divine revelation and even historical verification, but who cannot demonstrate it. Their so-called revelations contain numerous unfulfilled prophecies and/or historical inaccuracies. Islam and many Christian cults, such as Mormonism and Jehovah's Witnesses, fall into this category.

2. The fanciful philosophical speculations of religious sages or gurus (known or unknown, dead or alive). Often their pronouncements are esoteric ("physical reality is an illusion"), violate the laws of logic ("there are many paths to God"), and contradict normal human experience ("people are innately divine"). In all cases, these claims are unverifiable. Examples include Eastern religions, Hinduism and Buddhism, and their numerous New Age clones.

3. The wholly subjective opinions of self-appointed seers who don't even try to verify their claims beyond private, often mystical, religious experiences: "God appeared to me and said . . ." "People are laughing uncontrollably and barking like dogs—the Holy Spirit is moving in a new and powerful way!" These so-called religious experiences have spawned numerous strange beliefs and weird behaviors that are beyond the bounds of orthodoxy. Although many claim to be Christian, none can be justified biblically.[3]

Defending the Resurrection

Unquestionably, from what we've seen, only Christians have a holy Book that can be checked out and verified. In terms of apologetics, the question that needs to be examined now is, what is the most important thing the Bible teaches? What biblical doctrine is foremost on the apologist's agenda?

Romans 1:4 says that Jesus "was declared with power to be the Son of God by his resurrection from the dead." In Acts 17:31 Paul writes that God has given "proof" that Jesus will judge the world "by raising him from the dead." Elsewhere the apostle Paul writes that if Christ has not been resurrected, our faith is futile; we are still in our sins (unsaved) and "are to be pitied more than all men" (see 1 Cor. 15:17–19).

In light of these three passages, it's plain to see that the resurrection of Jesus Christ is the central proof that He is both God and Savior. And if Jesus is God and Savior, His words must be the very words of God. His instructions on salvation, ethical behavior, and how to live a more abundant life in the here and now are dependable.

In sum, if the Bible is the fundamental issue to defend in terms of establishing the authenticity and authority of Christianity, certainly the Resurrection is the foremost doctrine to defend in terms of justifying our faith in Jesus Christ.

The Logic of It All

I want to put what we've been looking at in a series of syllogisms. Doing this will help to make these important principles clear, and it will also show how to apply the facts in a systematic defense of apologetics. First, we saw the need to establish the divine authorship of Scripture:

Only God can write an infallible book. (premise 1)

The Bible is an infallible book. (premise 2)

Therefore, the Bible is the Word of God. (conclusion)

Now in a valid argument, the conclusion has to be true if the premises are true. What if the syllogism looked like this:

Only God can write an infallible book. (premise 1)

Engaging the Closed Minded is an infallible book. (premise 2)

Therefore, *Engaging the Closed Minded* is the Word of God. (conclusion)

What's wrong here? Obviously, premise two is in error. No human can write an infallible book. Hence, the conclusion must be wrong.

The apologist's task, then, is to demonstrate that the premises in a syllogism are true. If we do that, the conclusion must be true as long as it follows from the premises.

Let's return to the original syllogism:

Only God can write an infallible book. (premise 1)

The Bible is an infallible book. (premise 2)

Therefore, the Bible is the Word of God. (conclusion)

Premise 1 is essentially self-evident. No book written by a human is infallible. If an infallible book exists, only God could write it (inspire its authorship). Because no human being can submit an infallible book, few people will object to premise one. So we'll focus on premise two: The Bible is an infallible book. Here's where objections will occur. Most unbelievers will disagree with premise two. So our apologetic task is to muster evidence to support it. Once we verify premise two, the conclusion *must follow*: The Bible is the Word of God.

What evidence do we have to support premise 2? Here I must refer the reader to my book *Defending Your Faith,* or other introductory books on apologetics. Space prevents listing them here. What investigation will reveal, as pointed out above, is that the evidence supporting the truthfulness and reliability of Scripture is overwhelming. Premise 2 can easily be verified through the evidences of apologetics.

With the divine authorship of the Bible established, we have a basis for defending the authenticity of the Resurrection. The Resurrection, as Scripture makes clear, proves the deity of Jesus Christ. Hence, if the Bible is truthful, the Resurrection is a historical fact, and Jesus Christ is God. And if Jesus is God, then He speaks the truth of God concerning salvation and other issues. Here's the argument in syllogistic form:

Only God can write an infallible book. (premise 1)

The Bible is an infallible book. (premise 2)

Therefore, the Bible is the Word of God. (conclusion)

Only God can raise someone from the dead. (premise 1)

The Bible states that Jesus raised Himself from the dead—John 2:19; 10:17–18. (premise 2)

Therefore, Jesus is God. (conclusion)

Jesus as God speaks only truth. (premise 1)

Jesus says people are saved only through Him. (premise 2)

Therefore, Jesus is the only Savior. (conclusion)

Notice the progression of this logical argument. It forms an apologetic method for proving all Christian truth-claims.

First, we demonstrate the reliability and truthfulness of Scripture, thus establishing the Bible's authority as God's Word.

Second, we demonstrate that the Bible clearly teaches that Jesus Christ is God. This is proven (among other ways) by His resurrection from the dead.

Third, since Jesus is God, He speaks the words of God. Although

Jesus says many things vital to the human race, the most important thing He says is that salvation is only through Him (John 14:6; Acts 4:12).

What needs to be seen is that the last two syllogisms are true only if the first syllogism is true. And the first syllogism is true only if the Bible is true. Thus, the foundational task of apologetics is to prove the reliability and authenticity of the Bible.

This method moves step by step from an initial presupposition (which we prove evidentially: The Bible is divine revelation, infallible, and authoritative) to an inescapable conclusion: Jesus Christ is Lord and Savior.

This same technique—resting the defense of Christian truth-claims squarely on the authenticity of Scripture—is the procedure applied by several well-known Christian apologists. Here are three examples:

Dr. John Warwick Montgomery applies it in his resurrection argument:

1. On the basis of accepted principles of textual and historical analysis, the gospel records are found to be trustworthy historical documents—primary source evidence for the life of Christ.
2. In these records Jesus exercises divine prerogatives and claims to be God in human flesh; and He rests His claims on His forthcoming resurrection.
3. In all four gospels Christ's bodily resurrection is described in minute detail; Christ's resurrection evidences His deity.
4. The fact of the Resurrection cannot be discounted on *a priori*, philosophical grounds; miracles are impossible only if one defines them as such—but such a definition rules out proper historical investigation.
5. If Christ is God, then He speaks the truth concerning the absolute divine authority of the Old Testament and the soon-to-be-written New Testament, concerning His death for the sins of the world, and concerning the nature of man and of history.
6. It follows from the preceding that all biblical assertions bearing on a philosophy of history are to be regarded

ealed truth, and that all human attempts at
cal interpretation are to be judged for truth-value
on the basis of their harmony with scriptural revelation.[4]

Dr. Norman Geisler, in his apologetic textbook, *Christian Apologetics,*
uses this method to demonstrate that Jesus is the Son of God:

> The basic logic of the apologetic for Christianity
> is: (1) The New Testament is a historically reliable
> record of the life, teachings, death, and resurrec-
> tion of Jesus Christ . . .; (2) Jesus taught that he was
> God Incarnate . . .; (3) Jesus proved to be God In-
> carnate by fulfilling Old Testament prophecy, by a
> miraculous life, and by rising from the grave. . . .
> Therefore, Jesus of Nazareth is Deity.[5]

Likewise, R. C. Sproul, in his book *Reason to Believe,* uses a similar procedure to demonstrate the infallibility of Scripture:

> The case for the infallibility of Scripture proceeds
> along both deductive and inductive lines. It moves
> from the premise of general trustworthiness to the
> conclusion of infallibility. The reasoning proceeds
> as follows:
>
> Premise A— The Bible is a basically reliable and
> trustworthy document.
> Premise B— On the basis of this reliable document
> we have sufficient evidence to believe
> confidently that Jesus Christ is the Son
> of God.
> Premise C— Jesus Christ, being the Son of God, is
> an infallible authority.
> Premise D— Jesus Christ teaches that the Bible is
> more than generally trustworthy; it is
> the very Word of God.
> Premise E— The word, in that it comes from God,
> is utterly trustworthy because God is
> utterly trustworthy.

Conclusion—On the basis of the infallible authority
of Jesus Christ, the church believes the
Bible to be utterly trustworthy, i.e.,
infallible.[6]

Although Montgomery, Geisler, and Sproul are dealing with
somewhat different apologetic issues, you can see the similarities in
their approaches. All three systems contain two essential ingredients.

First, they all employ logical argumentation to reach an inescapable conclusion. Second, all three base their systems of
apologetics on the reliability and authenticity of Scripture. They
recognize that a successful apologetic system depends on the authority of the Bible as God's Word.

In terms of logical consistency, notice that all three apologists are
careful to avoid begging the question (i.e., that the conclusion is
valid because the premises assume it in advance). In other words,
their arguments don't move back and forth from Jesus verifying
the Bible to the Bible verifying Jesus—circular reasoning. Instead,
each argument claims that the Bible is a historically reliable, trustworthy document. Implicit in this claim is the existence of compelling, objective, non-biblical evidences. The premises are not merely
assumed; they can be proven. This is not circular reasoning.

Before moving on, I want point out that the apologetics issues
you encounter will not always focus on the reliability of the Bible.
Unbelievers harbor numerous concerns, obstacles to faith. It may
be they believe that evolution destroys Christianity because it
supposedly refutes the existence of God. They may practice another religious belief. Perhaps they are struggling with a philosophical issue such as the so-called "problem of evil." Or perhaps
it's a theological issue such as the eternal destiny of the heathen.

These matters may cause an unbeliever to reject the Bible out-
right and refuse to examine evidence for its truthfulness and reliability. If so, we will have to provide other evidences that they
will accept. For example, an evolutionist will likely need to see
scientific evidence supporting creation rather than evidence supporting the Bible, even though the Bible teaches creation. Nevertheless, since the Christian position in all matters rests firmly on
the authority of God's Word, most apologetic issues will eventually lead to a discussion of the authenticity of the Bible.

When this happens, our evangelism should begin to move away from apologetics and toward law and gospel. In other words, once we have established the authority of Scripture by proving its reliability and truthfulness, we confront the unbeliever with the gospel—and the consequences of rejecting it (law). The authority of Scripture is not only the fundamental issue of apologetics, it's also the premier point of contact leading to a gospel presentation.

One final thought. I'm not saying that we can trust the Bible only to the degree that we can prove it's true. That's not my point. Christians are justified in accepting the truth and authority of the Bible on its own merits. The Bible stands alone.

But we must understand that unbelievers do not have the witness of the indwelling Holy Spirit. According to 1 Corinthians 2:14, the unsaved person is not able to understand spiritual things. The apostle Paul writes, "The man without the Spirit does not accept the things that come from the Spirit of God, for they are foolishness to him, and he cannot understand them, because they are spiritually discerned."

If an unbeliever rejects the Bible off-the-cuff, it does no good to defend our beliefs by saying, "Well the Bible says . . ." We must provide evidence that demonstrates the Bible is true in order to create an environment in which the unbeliever will listen to the Bible's teachings.

And if the unbeliever will not consider evidence that confirms the Bible's truthfulness? Then we provide evidence he *will* accept. As Kreeft and Tacelli point out,

> [F]or many years early Christian apologists and church fathers argued quite effectively for Christianity without even *having* the New Testament Scriptures as authoritatively defined, since the canon was not established until generations later. And down through the centuries many people have in fact been led to belief—at least belief in a Creator God and in the *possibility* of salvation—through rational arguments not based on Scripture.[7]

In fact, as they suggest, it is sometimes easier to prove something other than the authority of Scripture first, like the existence of God or the deity of Christ, "where arguments can be simple, short and clear in a way that the arguments for the authority of Scripture can never be."[8]

Endnotes

1. Dan Story, *Defending Your Faith* (Grand Rapids: Kregel, 1997).
2. Dan Story, *Christianity on the Offense* (Grand Rapids: Kregel, 1998), chap. 6.
3. See Hank Hanegraaff, *Counterfeit Revival* (Dallas: Word, 1997).
4. John Warwick Montgomery, *The Shape of the Past* (Minneapolis, Minn.: Bethany House, 1975), 138–39.
5. Norman Geisler, *Christian Apologetics* (Grand Rapids: Baker, 1987), 329.
6. R. C. Sproul, *Reason to Believe* (Grand Rapids: Zondervan, 1982), 30–31.
7. Peter Kreeft and Ronald K. Tacelli, *Handbook of Christian Apologetics* (Downers Grove, Ill.: InterVarsity, 1994), 204.
8. Ibid.

4

Offensive Apologetics

In this chapter we will discuss what I believe is the most valuable and useful apologetic tactic you can learn. If you understand it, and if you apply it, I guarantee that you will increase your effectiveness in apologetics dramatically. The whole concept is summed up beautifully in Proverbs 18:17: "The first to present his case seems right, till another comes forward and questions him."

Those fifteen words describe concisely a fundamental truth: The arguments and assumptions that unbelievers bring to religious issues can sound truly convincing—*until* we pause a moment, think about what's being said, and then question such statements. Remarkably, when we do this, an unbeliever's arguments fall apart almost every time.

Anyone who lives an active Christian life, that is, anyone who is not too embarrassed or intimidated to let people know he or she is a believer, will be called upon to defend his or her faith. It's one of the ironies of the modern world that Christians must continually demonstrate that what they believe to be true *is true*. Christians are always put on the defensive.

It shouldn't be this way. Why? Because Christians are the ones who possess the truth, not unbelievers. We are the ones with a grasp on reality as it really exists. We are the ones who can demonstrate the legitimacy of our truth-claims. Unbelievers—not Christians—are the ones who should defend their worldview.

Our goal in this chapter is to learn how to be the challenger rather than the challenged in religious discussions. In other words, we will investigate how to turn the tide, so to speak, on unbelievers, removing the burden of proof from Christians and placing it on non-Christians.

Two Apologetics Approaches

It should be clear by now that the task of Christian apologetics is to identify misbeliefs and remove them as obstacles to faith. The goal is to compel unbelievers to reevaluate their anti-Christian assumptions in light of the evidence for the veracity of Christianity. This is "evidential" apologetics, and it works on the premise that the weight of evidence will always support Christianity and always refute contradicting beliefs.

There are two ways to identify these misbeliefs and to remove them as obstacles to faith. The traditional approach to evidential apologetics is to confront objections to Christianity one-by-one, as unbelievers raise them, and supply the proper Christian response, sometimes supported by non-biblical evidences. This is often referred to as "negative" apologetics, although I prefer to call it *defensive* apologetics. There's really nothing negative about it. Christians are simply defending their beliefs by responding to challenges to their faith.

Defensive apologetics is a valuable and long-standing apologetic approach, and it is crucial for overcoming barriers that hinder an unbeliever from considering Christianity as a world and life view. Its intention—and it often succeeds—is to clear the road for a gospel presentation.

But there is another apologetic strategy that we will examine in this chapter. In this approach, rather than defending our beliefs, we challenge unbelievers to defend *their* beliefs. This is "positive" apologetics or what I prefer to call *offensive* apologetics. I don't mean offensive as in bad taste, but offensive as in a football game. We become the aggressors. We force the unbeliever to take the defensive position and account for *his* religious or philosophical beliefs. In this approach, the "evidence" for Christianity becomes the unbeliever's inability to defend his worldview. Christianity is supported by default.

How do we do this? As Proverbs 18:17 instructs, we ask questions. First, we listen carefully to an unbeliever's opinion on a particular issue. In doing so, we identify inaccurate data, inconsistencies, and, especially, hidden assumptions. Then we ask for a response to these errors by questioning them. This places the burden of proof over disagreements on the unbeliever; it forces him to explain what he believes, why he believes it, and to justify it. Let me illustrate this.

I once had a discussion with a non-Christian friend who claimed that God is a vengeful deity and that the Bible is one of the "bloodiest" books ever written. He based this view on God's instructions to the Israelites in the Old Testament to kill every man, woman, child, and animal in the Canaanite nations they entered to possess (see, for example, Josh. 6:21).

Using offensive apologetics, I responded by identifying the unbeliever's hidden assumptions and questioning them. For example, my friend *assumed* that God destroyed the Canaanite nations without just cause. He *assumed* that the nations were not worthy of such treatment. He *assumed* that God's judgment was too harsh. He *assumed* that the Canaanite children were innocent and did not deserve such treatment.

After I identified these hidden assumptions, I then challenged them by asking pertinent questions, such as:

"Why do you think God was unfair?" (Obviously my friend didn't know that God had given the Canaanites centuries to repent—see Genesis 15:16 and Revelation 2:18–23.)

"What do you know about these people that makes you believe they didn't deserve such harsh treatment?" (He didn't realize how utterly depraved, detestable, and rebellious the Canaanites were—see Deuteronomy 9:4–5 and 18:9–12.)

"What makes you think that the children were treated unfairly?" (Did he realize that children learn their ethical behavior from their parents and culture? It's almost certain that the Canaanite children would grow up as wicked and perverted as their elders and deserve judgment every bit as much. While it is not possible to deal with this particular issue here in detail, it seems clear from many Bible passages that there is such a thing as an "age of accountability." Physical death is not as disastrous as spiritual death.)

When unbelievers fail to account for their erroneous assumptions or indicate they haven't considered our questions before and aren't prepared to respond, the door is open to give the Christian perspective on the subject at hand.

Do you see how this works? It's a shift in our tactics from defense to offense. It's approaching a religious discussion from a position that is adversarial rather than defensive. Once this technique becomes part of your arsenal, once it becomes a natural response, you'll automatically ask challenging questions as part of your strategy of apologetics.

This technique is contrary to our normal tendency to become defensive when our faith is challenged—to argue our point of view. At first blush, it may even seem counterproductive because we aren't providing an immediate answer to an unbeliever's challenge. But it's not counterproductive. It's a highly effective tactic. Like defensive apologetics, offensive apologetics is designed to help unbelievers see why Christians are Christians and open the door for a gospel presentation.

I can't emphasize how effective—even revolutionary—this approach is. When I've taught this concept in classes on apologetics, students tell me it has helped them tremendously—even with people to whom they have been applying defensive apologetics. Unbelievers are confounded to find themselves unable to substantiate their non-Christian beliefs or their misconceptions about Christianity. They've never been forced to do so before. In many instances, this leads to a willingness to reconsider the Christian position.

This forceful and effective apologetic technique is called the *Socratic Method,* and it's based on the dialectical style of the philosopher Socrates.

Socrates

Socrates (470–399 B.C.) was an early Greek philosopher. Although he apparently wrote no treatises himself, we know about him and his teachings through his famed student, Plato. Plato recounts that Socrates employed a method of argumentation that relied on "patient questioning" in order to bring a student to the apprehension of truth without actually teaching the truth itself.

Frederick Copleston, in *A History of Philosophy,* describes this technique:

> What was Socrates' practical method? It took the
> form of "dialectic" [a systematic examination of

ideas to test them for validity] or conversation. He would get into conversation with someone and try to elicit from him his ideas on some subject. For instance, he might profess his ignorance of what courage really is, and ask the other man if he had any light on the subject. Or Socrates would lead the conversation in that direction, and when the other man had used the word "courage," Socrates would ask him what courage is, professing his own ignorance and desire to learn. His companion had used the word, therefore he must know what it meant. When some definition or description had been given him, Socrates would profess his great satisfaction, but would intimate that there were one or two little difficulties which he would like to see cleared up [sounds like television's Colombo, doesn't it?]. Accordingly he asked questions, letting the other man do most of the talking, but keeping the course of conversation under his control, and so would expose the inadequacy of the proposed definition of courage. The other would fall back on a fresh or modified definition, and so the process would go on, with or without final success.[1]

By asking specific questions that challenged his students' assumptions, Socrates lead them into a kind of self-discovery. They concluded for themselves the error of their existing beliefs and went on to accept a new truth or a different conclusion.

In a similar fashion, the Socratic Method of argumentation provides Christian evangelists with a means of controlling the conversation in apologetic encounters. It compels the unbeliever to reconsider the inadequacy of his own beliefs—or his misconceptions about Christianity.

This technique works on the premise that non-Christians hold certain presuppositions (assumptions) basic to their religious or secular beliefs that are in error. In other words, their beliefs are wrong because the assumptions they take for granted are wrong.

By asking challenging questions that help unbelievers see this for themselves, we have a much better chance of getting them to reconsider the Christian position on the issue at hand than if we just provided evidence to support our own position and never really forced them to examine theirs.

Summary

In a moment we'll look at the kinds of Socratic questions we can ask, but first let me summarize the value of offensive apologetics.

Asking challenging questions helps unbelievers to reconsider Christianity for two reasons: First, their existing religious or secular worldviews can't be substantiated. In other words, unbelievers discover that they are unable to defend what they believe. They can't muster evidence to support their view the way we can. When they see this, we point out that we *can* confirm our views. This should cause fair-minded people to reconsider their own presuppositions and listen to ours.

Second, unbelievers see that their view of Christianity is erroneous. Non-Christians frequently harbor misconceptions about what the Bible teaches and misunderstandings of what Christians actually believe. Their opinions, more often than not, are byproducts of our secular culture—not the result of personal investigation. Often unbelievers are merely parroting what they've read or heard somewhere. For example, many non-Christians believe that the Bible is full of contradictions and that it contains unscientific data and historical inaccuracies. All of these misconceptions are the fruit of an uninformed and prejudiced secular culture.

If unbelievers see that what they thought was true about Christianity is false, perhaps they will be more willing to reconsider Christianity. They will allow us to explain what is true about Christianity in terms of our beliefs and practices—especially concerning Jesus and salvation.

So offensive apologetics not only challenges the unbelievers' worldviews, but it also challenges their misconceptions about Christianity. Since Christianity is not what they think it is, should they not reconsider it?

How the Socratic Method Works

Christians believe that all spiritual truth and moral truth is tightly bound to Scripture. If this is true, it follows that non-

Christian religions and secular philosophies will eventually lead practitioners to a dead end. They may contain sparks of religious or moral truth, but the full light of truth will be absent. Pursuing spiritual truth in non-Christian religions will always end in failure. As Francis Schaeffer put it:

> [I]n reality no one can live logically according to his own non-Christian presuppositions. . . . [R]egardless of a man's system, he has to live in God's world. If he were consistent to his non-Christian presuppositions he would be separated from the real universe. . . .[2]

Schaeffer tells us that only Christianity accurately portrays reality as it exists. Any worldview other than Christianity will inevitably prove itself to be inconsistent and, hence, erroneous if pressed far enough. Schaeffer suggests how to test this:

> We ought not first try to move a man away from what he should deduce from his position but towards it. . . . We try to move him in the natural direction in which his presuppositions would take him. We are then pushing him towards the place where he ought to be, had he not stopped short.[3]

What Schaeffer is suggesting is essentially the Socratic Method. We encourage an unbeliever to follow his religious presuppositions to their logical conclusion. When he does this, the unbeliever will inevitably discover that his religious beliefs are untenable. They not only break down in terms of coherence, but also they are impossible to live with consistently without being "separated from the real universe." Hence, they are incapable of leading to spiritual truth. Some illustrations will be helpful here.

Christian Science teaches that evil and sickness are illusions.[4] Here's the line of reasoning. If all things are created by God, and if God said that His creation is good, then it follows that what we perceive as evil and sickness can't exist—they're illusions. On the surface this would seem to make some sense, but let's follow the advice of Proverbs 18:17 and "question" it. Does it *really* make sense?

There are many theological problems with this dogma, but we'll look at it from a purely pragmatic point of view. The problem is, no one—including Christian Scientists—can live consistently with the claim that evil and sickness are illusions. People who adhere to this doctrine and get a fatal disease die—unless they get medical aid. But if they get medical aid, they are demonstrating by their actions that the dogma is false. Likewise, we need only pick up a newspaper to see that evil is real. Examples are not even necessary.

If so-called illusions must be treated as reality, to claim that evil and sickness are illusions is meaningless. No one can demonstrate that evil and sickness are unreal because we live in a universe that screams their reality. Everyone lives as if evil and sickness are real. Followed to its logical conclusion, the Christian Scientists' claim that evil and sickness are illusions falls into a mire of inconsistencies, contradictions, and confusion.

In a similar fashion, New Age adherents insist that man is innately good—actually, divine—and that what Christians call sin is merely a response to a lack of right information about how one should behave. Once people realize their divine potential and gain right information, they will make correct choices, and sin will vanish.

But again, this presupposition flies in the face of how people really behave. People do have right information about many things and still make wrong choices. People smoke knowing it can cause cancer. They eat fatty foods knowing they can cause heart disease. People cheat on their taxes and their spouses when they know these things are wrong. They pollute the environment and stockpile nuclear weapons knowing both can unleash doomsday.

Moreover, people are not inherently good. If they were, at the very least we would see signs of this in small children before they are tainted by worldly values. Yet even toddlers exhibit signs of an innate tendency to sin. We have to train our children not to hit, steal, and sass—they do these evil things naturally.

And what about the New Agers' claim to divinity? If anyone can exhibit a single attribute of deity, that is, if anyone can perform a single supernatural act that is clearly "divine" in nature— well, I'd pay to see it. You see, these presuppositions, tested in the real world, fail. They cannot be substantiated by objective evidence or by what we observe in human nature.

Here's a final example of a worldview presupposition leading, as Schaeffer says, away from "the real universe." Proponents of religious pluralism claim that all religions teach essentially the same great truths. Thus, all religions are equally valid paths up the mountain to "God." But is this possible? The answer is no. It can't be possible because it violates the most fundamental law of logic, the law of *noncontradiction*.

This basic law of logic states that something cannot be two different things at the same time and in the same sense ("A" cannot be both "A" and "non-A" at the same time). It can't be daytime and nighttime outside at the same time and in the same spot. I can't be eating breakfast at a local cafe at six A.M. and sleeping in my bed at the same time.

The fact is, all world religions are clearly different in their essential beliefs. The nature of God, concepts of salvation, and other major doctrines vary greatly among the world's religions. If two religions teach opposing views on these essentials, they can't both be right. They may both be wrong, but only one can be correct. God can't be the impersonal, unknowable "It" of pantheism and the personal, knowable God of Christianity. He can't be the sole God of the universe as Christians, Jews, and Muslims teach, and share the universe with a multitude of other gods as polytheism teaches. In short, followed to its logical conclusion, the fundamental presupposition of religious pluralism—that all religions are true—is logically impossible.

Asking Socratic Questions

This brings us to application. How do we persuade unbelievers, such as Christian Scientists, New Age practitioners, or religious pluralists, to critically examine their presuppositions? I believe the Socratic Method provides an effective way of doing this. By asking the right questions, we can force unbelievers to confront their beliefs and to justify them.

Let's begin by listing some of the *kinds* of questions we can ask.

Do they have proof? Is their source reliable?
- "How do you know that?"
- "What evidence do you have for that?"

"Why do you believe that?"
"Where did you learn that?"
- "On what authority do you base your view?"
- "Aren't you taking . . . for granted?"

Clarification or elaboration:
- "What do you mean by that?"
- "I don't follow you, tell me more."
- "Can you give me an example?"
- "You seem to be contradicting yourself. You said earlier . . ."
- "What difference does it make?"
- "How can . . . ?"

Consequences:
- "What happens if you're wrong?"
- "Are you willing to risk salvation rather than . . . ?"
- "Have you ever considered . . . ?"

Secondary issues that result from hidden assumptions:
- "What you say creates another problem."
- "That raises another question."
- "Then what about this . . . ?"
- "In light of what you believe, how would you explain . . . ?"
- "How do you account for . . . ?"

Let's apply some of these kinds of questions to the three worldviews examined above (Christian Science, New Age, and religious pluralism) and also to evolution. I'll add a few other examples:

- "How do you know that evil and sickness are illusions?"
- "What evidence do you have that people are actually divine?"
- "Where did you learn that all religions are true?"
- "What happens if you're wrong, and all religions don't lead to God?"

- "Are you willing to risk salvation rather than check out Christianity?"
- "Why do you believe in evolution? Have you ever checked out creation? Aren't you taking for granted that evolution is true?"
- "Why does belief in evolution discount Christianity or salvation through Jesus Christ?"
- "How can order come from disorder?"
- "How can life come from nonlife?"
- "How can something come from nothing?"
- "If Jesus didn't die and rise from the grave, how do you account for the existence of the Christian church and the changed lives of His disciples?"
- "In light of what you believe, if it's a myth that Christ died and rose from the dead, how do you account for the untold thousands of Christians who were willing die for their faith?"

You will be surprised at the responses to these kinds of questions. Most non-Christians take their beliefs, or their worldview presuppositions, for granted. (Of course, so do Christians. But as I've shown elsewhere, Christians can justify their presuppositions with testable, objective evidence.[5]) It's an eye-opener when unbelievers discover that they can't justify what they believe. Likewise, unbelievers are often surprised to learn that what they assume to be true about Christianity is wholly false. Many times this will leave the door wide open for us to explain the true Christian position on the topic under discussion.

Boomerang Questions

Another Socratic approach is to ask unbelievers the same kinds of questions they ask Christians: "How do *you* explain the presence of pain and suffering?" "How do *you* know your holy book is true revelation?" "How do *you* know your religion is true when it contradicts other religions that also claim to be true?" and so on. As Alister McGrath says, "Too often, those who ask critical questions of evangelicalism fail to realize that those same critical questions need to be addressed within their own ranks as well."[6]

Let me illustrate this technique by presenting a series of hypothetical conversations. Notice that all the Christian responses are designed to place the burden of proof on the unbeliever by challenging her to respond to the very issues she raises:

Unbeliever: "You Christians can't prove what you believe!"
Christian: "Then you prove what you believe!"

Unbeliever: "How do you know the Bible is true?"
Christian: "How do you know it's not true?"

Unbeliever: "The Bible is full of contradictions!"
Christian: "What contradictions?"

Unbeliever: "If the Christian God exists, how do you account for the existence of evil and suffering?"
Christian: "If God doesn't exist, what is the solution to evil and suffering?"

Unbeliever: "I think belief in God is a psychological crutch for weak people. What proof do you have that God even exists?"
Christian: "I think atheism is a psychological crutch to get off the hook in terms of accountability to God. What proof do you have that the evidence for God's existence is false?"

Unbeliever: "Christians are so narrow-minded. You only think your religion is true!"
Christian: "Don't you believe what you say is true? Does that make you narrow-minded? Does being narrow-minded automatically make something untrue?"

Unbeliever: "I think people are free to decide their own moral standards."
Christian: "Then you think it was okay for Hitler to massacre 6 million Jews?"

Unbeliever:	"The Christian God is harsh and vindictive. Look how He annihilated whole cities in the Old Testament."
Christian:	"Why do you think God is cruel and unfair to punish a wicked and perverted people who were warned for centuries to repent and yet continued to blaspheme God, worship pagan deities, engage in deviant, forbidden sexual acts in the name of religion, and even sacrifice their children to false gods?"
Unbeliever:	"I could never follow a God who sends people to hell just because they don't worship Him as you Christians do."
Christian:	"You mean you're willing to go to hell just because God doesn't act the way you think He should?"
Unbeliever:	"What makes you think Christianity is true when it contradicts my religious beliefs?"
Christian:	"How do you know your religion is true when it contradicts Christianity? Can you prove your religion is true?"
Unbeliever:	"How do you know Jesus really speaks for God?"
Christian:	"What evidence do you have that Charles Taze Russell [or Joseph Smith or Muhammad] speaks for God? How does he prove it?"
Unbeliever:	"If a woman wants an abortion, it's her right to do whatever she wants with her own body."
Christian:	"If a baby is a human being, why wouldn't it have the same right to live as the mother?"
Unbeliever:	"We don't need a God to set standards of good and evil. People can make their own moral choices."
Christian:	"Then if I say infanticide is acceptable, would you agree?"
Unbeliever:	"Science disproves miracles like the Resurrection."
Christian:	"Aren't miracles like the Resurrection historical events? How can science disprove anything in history?"

Unbeliever: "I don't believe God exists."

Christian: "If there was a time when nothing existed, what would be here now if there is no God? What I mean is, if God doesn't exist, how did nature come into being? Can something create itself? Can something come from nothing?"

Do you see what's being done here? Rather than defending our beliefs, we are challenging unbelievers to account for their beliefs. We are shifting the burden of proof away from Christianity to the non-Christian.

The purpose of these kinds of questions, then, is to point out problems that the unbeliever cannot easily resolve and has likely never considered. People seldom think through their beliefs. Religious and ethical presuppositions (assumptions) are usually taken for granted as truth. The right questions force unbelievers to rethink their beliefs. When they do this, they are frequently more willing to listen to Christian alternatives.

Bite-Sized Chunks

The Socratic Method reduces complicated issues to a manageable size. Many of the problems raised by non-Christians are simple to state but complex in nature. In many witnessing encounters, we simply don't have the time—or perhaps even the knowledge—to give an adequate response. For example, consider this popular argument against the existence of God:

> If God is as all-loving and all-powerful, as you Christians claim, He wouldn't allow evil and suffering. But evil and suffering exist. Therefore, God is either not all-loving and doesn't care that people suffer, or He's not all-powerful and can't stop it. Either way, God doesn't exist as you Christians believe.

Entire books have been written in response to this argument, called the "problem of evil."[7] It's impossible to give an adequate reply to such a complex and emotion-laden issue during a coffee break at work or a casual encounter at a party. But the Socratic

Method allows us to give a reasonable response by shifting the issue back to the unbeliever. Our reply can be something like this:

> You've identified one of the biggest dilemmas confronting the human race, regardless of one's religious belief. Not only Christians but also people of all religions and philosophies—even atheists—must deal with this issue of human suffering and evil. I believe that the Christian solution is the only logical and sustainable response to this problem, and I'd love to get together when we have more time and explain it [or, "I have a book I can lend you, and we can discuss the matter after you read it"]. But for now let me give you something to think about.
>
> If God *doesn't* exist, what is the solution to evil and human suffering? It's easy to blame God, so let's remove Him from the equation. What's left? Can you think of a solution to evil and suffering without God?

The unbeliever will have one of two responses. (1) He will offer another solution. But with further investigation, he'll discover that there is no better solution to the problem of evil than the Christian one. No other religion or philosophy, including pantheism, dualism, secular humanism, naturalism, postmodernism, and New Age thought can offer a solution to the problem of evil. They all either ignore it or accept it, but they don't solve it.[8]

(2) The unbeliever will admit that there is no solution. But then we've won the argument, because he's inadvertently admitting that only God can solve the problem of evil.

Here's another response to the problem of evil, applying the Socratic Method:

> It is true that God is all-loving and able to stop pain and suffering right now if He wants to. But it's also true that He chooses not to. Instead of rejecting God, wouldn't it be wiser to ask "Why?" If

> God can stop evil and suffering, and doesn't, there
> must be a reason.

In other words, why throw the baby out with the bath water? If God exists, there must be a reason why he allows human (and animal) suffering. This opens the door to the Christian explanation of the Fall—and, more importantly, salvation.

In these two scenarios, we've taken an issue that many unbelievers consider irrefutable proof for the non-existence of the Christian God and forced them to reevaluate their position. When non-Christians discover for themselves that alternative solutions fail, they may be willing to listen to the Christian answer.

Let me tie this all together. Applied to this difficult issue, the Socratic Method does four things. First, it allows us to give a response when time restricts a full reply. Second, it clears away peripheral issues and gets right to the heart of the problem: Is there a solution to the problem of evil without God? The answer is no. Whatever the solution to the problem of evil is, it must include God, or it doesn't exist. One cannot reject God and still come to terms with the problem of evil. Third, we have challenged the erroneous anti-Christian assumptions that God either (a) can't solve the problem of evil, (b) is the cause of it, or (c) doesn't exist. And fourth, we have opened the door for further dialogue—a witnessing opportunity.

Nonthreatening

There is still another benefit to using the Socratic Method. As I've said, the goal of the Socratic Method is to get an unbeliever to conclude for himself, rather than being told, that his present religious or secular beliefs on a particular subject are inadequate. Because the unbeliever reaches this conclusion primarily on his own, we don't come across as trying to intellectually clobber an opponent.

The Socratic Method avoids a pitfall common in apologetic evangelism: raising the ire of non-Christians. Christians possess religious and moral truth and are able to muster considerable evidence to substantiate their claims. Without much difficulty, most Christian apologists can out argue most unbelievers at every turn. However, when people feel themselves shoved into a cerebral corner where there is no way out but to admit they're wrong, they seldom do so. Rather, they get angry. Or they shut down completely and refuse to debate any further. Or they cross their arms and irrationally reject the Christian view in spite of the evidences.

There's something in human nature that makes us hate to admit we're wrong, especially in a heated debate in front of our peers. The issue becomes more one of saving face than winning the argument. As Alister McGrath points out, "People find it difficult to change their minds if they are made to feel it is a win-or-lose situation. Bad apologetics creates the impression that changing your mind is equivalent to losing an argument. And nobody likes losing an argument—especially in public."[9]

The Socratic Method challenges unbelievers to reexamine their position without our hammering the Christian point of view down their throats. We're not lecturing; we're asking questions. It encourages unbelievers to accept the Christian solution through their own reasoning channels. It tactfully reveals that their own approach can't resolve the very dilemma with which they condemn Christianity. It gives them a way to admit defeat on their own terms.

Let me illustrate this principle. Suppose you are engaged in a discussion on creation versus evolution. Let's see how the defensive and offensive approaches differs:

> **Defensive:** Let's look at the evidence. There are no transitional fossils in the fossil record. Probability studies clearly prove that mutations—given the age of the earth in evolutionary terms—are unable to account for the development of higher species from primitive species. There's not a shred of evidence life arose from nonlife in some imaginary chemical soup that supposedly existed before life on earth. How can you maintain that creation is a Christian myth? The evidence proves evolution is a myth!

Now, lets apply this same information through the Socratic Method:

Offensive: Let me ask you a couple of questions about evolution. I'd like to see how your view explains a few things that I think the creation model explains more easily. For example, how do you account for the total absence in the fossil record of transitional fossils when evolution claims that one animal type, like reptiles, evolved into another animal type, like mammals? There are no half-reptile, half-mammal fossils, or half-dog, half-cat fossils, for that matter.

I understand that probability studies clearly demonstrate that the earth isn't old enough for mutations to account for the emergence of higher life forms from lower life forms? How then did higher life arise without a creator?

I've read recently that there is no known mechanism in nature that can cause life to spring from nonlife. How can evolution claim as fact that life arose from nonlife when there is no evidence to support it?

I'm not saying that unbelievers will never have a thoughtful response to our questions. They may very well. However, if unbelievers do have a rejoinder, it will always fall short of the Christian position in terms of supporting evidence. Remember, Christianity is truth. We will always have the correct solution to any conflicting worldview issue—we just have to know it.

Remember Your Goal

Finally, the Socratic Method is in harmony with the second commandment of good apologetics (see chap. 2). It can lead to a gospel presentation. After discussing the unbeliever's stand on relative ethics, the problem of evil, or creation, we can move the conversation to direct evangelism by asking this simple, unobtrusive question: "Do you understand, or know, what the Bible teaches in this area?"

Many unbelievers will admit they don't, and you can give the Christian view to a willing listener. If unbelievers say yes, ask them to explain. Likely they will present a distorted or popularized picture of what they think is the Christian view. Either way, the door is open for leading the conversation to a gospel presentation.

Endnotes

1. Frederick S. J. Copleston, *A History of Philosophy,* vol. 1 (New York: Doubleday, 1985), 106.
2. Francis A. Schaeffer, *The God Who Is There* (Downers Grove, Ill.: InterVarsity, 1968), 126.
3. Ibid., 127.
4. See Josh McDowell and Don Stewart, *Understanding the Cults* (San Bernardino, Calif.: Here's Life, 1982).
5. See Dan Story, *Defending Your Faith* (Grand Rapids: Kregel, 1997); and idem, *Christianity on the Offense* (Grand Rapids: Kregel, 1998).
6. Alister McGrath, *A Passion for Truth* (Downers Grove, Ill.: InterVarsity, 1996), 22.
7. See C. S. Lewis, *The Problem of Pain* (New York: Macmillan, 1962); and Norman L. Geisler, *The Roots of Evil,* 2d ed. (Dallas: Probe, 1989).
8. See Story, *Defending Your Faith,* chap. 13.
9. Alister McGrath, *Intellectuals Don't Need God, and Other Modern Myths* (Grand Rapids: Zondervan, 1993), 90.

5

Communicating Clearly

Teenagers of all generations use insider words that are known only to themselves. When my own kids were teenagers, it seemed as if they sometimes communicated on AM while my frequency was FM; my receiver didn't pick up their broadcasts. They spoke English—but of a peculiar kind. Words such as *rad* and *gnarly* and *boss* showered their sentences, and I frequently had to ask for a translation.

Perhaps there's a lesson here for evangelists and apologists. Could we be using words and expressions that are foreign to unbelievers? We should try to communicate the Christian messages of salvation and morality in everyday language—in words we're certain unbelievers will understand.

The Problem

Christianity is no longer the dominant worldview in Western culture. More and more we are reflecting the traits of a subculture within the larger framework of the secular world. We publish our own books. We read our own magazines. We attend our own colleges and universities. We use certain words and phrases to describe our beliefs and activities. And perhaps most damaging to evangelism, we prefer to associate only with other Christians.

Moreover, like teenagers of every generation, Christians converse in a particular jargon, "hang out" with their own peers, and socialize in ways that are attractive primarily to other Christians.

Evangelist Jim Petersen gives us a well-needed warning about this:

> Christians who keep to themselves, who do not experience a continuing influx of people just arriving from the dominion of darkness, soon surround themselves with their own subculture. Receiving no feedback from people fresh from the world, they forget what it's like out there. Peculiar language codes, behavioral patterns, and communication techniques emerge that only have meaning for the insider [Christians].[1]

In light of this, it's fitting that we spend some time discussing how to communicate with non-Christians. We want to learn how to say what needs to be said in a way that people will listen, understand, and accept.

Rules of the Game

"Be Quick to Listen, Slow to Speak" (James 1:19)

The first rule of good communication comes right from Scripture. James's admonition, applied to apologetics, is to listen before you respond. In any debate with an unbeliever, there is a tendency to anticipate what he is about to say, and to be thinking of our own response, rather than listening to what he actually is saying. We need to be good listeners. If we don't identify hidden assumptions, inaccurate data, misconceptions, or other obstacles to understanding and accepting Christianity, we cannot ask the kinds of challenging questions that will turn the conversation away from untruth to truth. A good listener does not interrupt to voice his opinion before the other person completes his thought.

Be Prepared

Using the Socratic Method demands that we know the Christian solution to the problems inherent in the unbeliever's position. If we don't know the subject at hand, we can't identify hidden assumptions, inaccurate data, or misconceptions.

Moreover, once an unbeliever concludes for herself that her

present view possesses fatal flaws, it's necessary to demonstrate that the Christian alternative is correct. Otherwise, the unbeliever may opt for still another erroneous worldview, and you are back to square one. It's impossible to be effective using the Socratic Method (or any apologetic tactic) without a background in evidential apologetics.

Fortunately, a good self-education in apologetics is available to all Christians. The answers to 99 percent of the questions unbelievers ask, and the arguments they present, can be found in many introductory books on apologetics.

Avoid Loaded Language

In conversing with unbelievers, it is essential to follow the apostle Paul's instructions in Colossians 4:6: "Let your conversation be always full of grace, seasoned with salt, so that you may know how to answer everyone." More often than not, at least initially, our sincerity, our tone of voice, and our ability and willingness to listen attentively and respectively will count as much in an apologetics encounter as what we say. This means that we must avoid loaded language, words and phrases that belittle, mock, or ridicule. As Kreeft and Tacelli point out,

> An argument in apologetics, when actually used in dialogue, is an extension of the arguer. The arguer's tone, sincerity, care, concern, listening and respect matter as much as his or her logic— probably more. The world was won for Christ not by arguments but by sanctity: "What you are speaks so loud, I can hardly hear what you say."[2]

Search Ministries produces an excellent workbook on lifestyle evangelism titled, *Connexions: Developing a Lifestyle of Evangelism Among Friends*. They make a similar point: "Only 7 percent of effective communication involves the actual words. Ninety-three percent of the communication process incorporates the non-verbal components. In other words, how you say what you say is critically important."[3]

In appendix three of the same workbook, Search Ministries offers the list of things to avoid saying, along with introductory comments, that appears on page 86.

Beware of these responses. When someone force-fully expresses a view which belittles or puts down your faith, emotions soar and it is easy to respond with these kinds of statements. Here are the discussion stiflers.

- It's a proven fact that . . .
- That's just the way it is.
- There's no question about . . .
- Only fools believe . . .
- (Using a condescending tone of voice) The Bible says . . .
- You don't know what you're talking about.
- That's ridiculous.
- Look at the evidence.
- That just doesn't fit the facts.
- You're not serious.
- Well, if you believe that, then . . .
- There's just no evidence for . . .
- That's been totally disproved.
- Give me a break; that was refuted years ago.
- Hey, if you believe that, you are committing intellectual suicide.
- That's a self-defeating argument; you've just said something that's impossible.
- You're being totally illogical.
- How can you even say that?[4]

All of us can probably add to this list. The message here is to avoid words and phrases that raise people's hackles rather than open their minds.

Use Everyday Language

Jim Petersen observes that Christian evangelists are "given to extremes. Either we say nothing and let an opportunity slip past us, or we say too much and drive people away."[5] I want to add a third communication problem: We don't use ordinary language. We use words and phrases that are understandable primarily just to other Christians. Let me illustrate how baffling this can be.

You invite a non-Christian friend to church who has never been before. Put yourself in her shoes and try to imagine what it's like.

First, let's look at prayer. She will notice an immediate change in the pastor's voice. He will sound more reverent and supplicatory than during the announcements. "Father," "Son," and "Holy Spirit" are used interchangeably. Phrases like, "bind Satan," "Lord, touch his body with your healing hand," "fill us with your Spirit," and many other strange-sounding (to her) utterances are spoken.

What word pictures do you think these phrases conjure up in an unbeliever's mind? Three Gods? A lassoed and cinched-up Satan? A bodily God with magic fingers? An apparition moving into a person's body?

Next, consider the songs we sing. Many of the lyrics will have no meaning to unbelievers because of the Christian metaphors being used: "the potter and the clay," "washed in His blood," "blind but now I see," and so on. Again, what strange images can these conjure up in the unchurched person's mind?

Then comes the sermon. Once again, you hear numerous unconventional expressions: "born again," "living sacrifice," "led by the Holy Spirit," and so on.

Now, I'm not saying these expressions shouldn't be used. They clearly communicate the intricacies of our faith as well as our feelings of love and gratitude toward God. We can't expect church services or home Bible studies not to use ordinary Christian vocabulary. Nor can pastors and teachers take the time to explain every word or concept that may sound foreign to an unbeliever.

Having said this, however, I do believe that Christians can and should be selective in the words and phrases they use when engaged in evangelism or apologetics. Indeed, some of the words we employ can convey an entirely different meaning to unbelievers than intended. For example, if I tell an unbeliever that I have the "gift" of teaching, will he really understand what I mean? He may think I went to college for free! If I say God "led" me to such and such a decision, he may wonder if I actually heard God speak. We need to use everyday language; we need to use synonyms; we need to define our terms.

Below are common Christian words and phrases that have clear and specific meanings to Christians but may sound strange and ambiguous to non-Christians or carry different meanings in the secular world. I have suggested alternative words, synonyms, phrases, or definitions that carry the same meanings but will be more understandable to non-Christians. The list is not exhaustive, and you should add to it yourself.

- "Believer" (Christian)
- "Fellowship" (getting together with other Christians)
- "Faith" (trusting God)
- "Spiritual warfare" (our struggles against sinful thoughts and temptations)
- "Praise music" (worshiping God through song)
- "Judged" (how God deals fairly with unbelievers)
- "Saved" (From what? Explain.)
- "Hell" (eternal separation from God)
- "Binding Satan" (praying to God to protect us from the evil forces in the world)
- "God spoke to me" (Explain how.)
- "Indwelt by the Holy Spirit" (God's Spirit, living in the hearts of Christians, empowering us for ministry and to resist sin)
- "Baptized by the Holy Spirit" (When we first believe, the Spirit of God empowers Christians to resist sin and to serve Him.)
- "Holy Ghost" (Boo! Use "Holy Spirit" or "Spirit of God," depending on context of discussion.)
- "Father" (Use "God" unless unbeliever is familiar with the concept of the Trinity.)
- "Son of God" (Use "Jesus" unless unbeliever understands the concept of Trinity.)
- "Gifts" (the strengths and talents God gives us to serve Him in particular ways)
- "Rapture" (believers alive when Jesus returns are taken directly to heaven without physical death)
- "Born again" (When we become Christians by receiving Jesus as our personal Lord and Savior, Jesus takes charge of our lives and we receive new, eternal natures that are empowered by God to obedience and faith.)
- "Resurrection" (Unbelievers need to understand that after death they will receive a physical body and not just a spiri-

tual, ghostly body. Be sure the unbeliever doesn't confuse resurrection with reincarnation.)

When you talk to non-Christians and use theological terms such as "atonement," "justification," "reconciliation," "redemption," "sanctification," "transformation," "Trinity," and so on, they too need to be defined. To most unbelievers, these words, when used in a Christian context, are as foreign as beta particles and quasars are to non-astronomers.

One final thought before moving on. Many Christians like to use theological words. Yet when it comes to defining them, they struggle to do so. They know their meanings more or less, but they can't readily articulate them. Learning to define these terms is a good exercise for developing your understanding of what they mean. If you don't understand these concepts yourself, you won't be able to explain them to unbelievers. Certainly, to be effective in apologetics and evangelism, we must understand—and be able to explain—our doctrines. I think C. S. Lewis is right when he says, "If, given patience and ordinary skill you cannot explain a thing to any sensible person whatever (provided he will listen), then you don't really understand it yourself."[6]

Use Word Pictures

Christians have always had the challenge of communicating the gospel to succeeding generations in a relevant and compelling way. Cultures are not static. They are living organisms that constantly undergo dynamic change. No time in history has undergone such radical changes within a single generation as ours. The world of the late 1990s is far different, in terms of ethics, religion, and social behavior, than the world of the late 1950s—a mere generation ago.

After nearly three centuries of Enlightenment thinking, where truth was seen as rational, objective, and attainable, Western culture is now abandoning this traditional "modernist" view of reality and is moving toward a "postmodernist" view where truth is relativistic, subjective, and unattainable.[7]

Today, communicating the gospel as a set of propositional statements of truth (truth that can be checked out and verified; truth that is applicable to everyone) is becoming increasingly ineffective.

While past generations of evangelists based their apologetic tactics on Enlightenment thinking—that is, they used the tools of logic and the scientific method for verifying truth—today's generation, which has not been raised in a modernist culture, is rejecting reason and objectivity in favor of feelings and experiences.[8] Communicating the gospel now will require a different approach.

Many apologists today suggest that we turn to storytelling. As British evangelist Nick Pollard puts it:

> [W]e can (and must) work within the methodology of postmodernism if we really are going to reach people in this culture. Two major characteristics of postmodernism are of particular importance to us in evangelism: (1) the emphasis on questioning and (2) the displacement of propositional truth in favor of stories. If we are to be effective within this postmodern culture, then, our evangelism must involve the appropriate use of questions and stories. This is not actually anything new; it is the way in which Jesus taught. He made use of questions, often answering one question with another [sounds Socratic]. And he told the greatest stores of all time.[9]

Some people are natural storytellers. They have the ability to take muddy, abstract concepts and recreate them into clear, understandable stories. Some of the most spellbinding and memorable portions of a good sermon are the creative illustrations that vividly drive home the crux of the message. We may forget the Bible passages and the finer doctrinal points, but we don't forget the stories that illustrate them.

Gary Smalley and John Trent in their book *The Language of Love,* refer to these illustrations as "word pictures." They are visual stories that provide insight and understanding into emotionally charged or intellectually complicated issues where raw data fails. The idea is to convey truth subjectively because cognitive communication is ineffective.

Smalley and Trent's book is orientated toward developing better communication skills among family members. But the principle they promote—illustrating truth through narrative stories—is a legitimate tool in apologetic evangelism. As the authors explain, "No matter who you are and what you do, you can't escape the need to communicate meaningfully with others. And without exception, we will run into the limitation of everyday expressions."[10]

In evangelism I see this to mean that there will be times when we just can't get our thoughts across using a purely rational approach or by creating an inventory of pertinent doctrinal or apologetic facts. There are people—especially the tender-minded—who will grasp biblical truths more easily through illustrations and personal testimonies than data. Let me illustrate this.

One of the key biblical principles that we must communicate accurately to unbelievers is God's grace in forgiveness; that is, we are justified (forgiven and made right in God's sight—saved) by grace, not by our good "works" (Eph. 2:8). This is weighty stuff for many unbelievers. It is difficult to understand because most people naturally believe they can "earn" forgiveness (and hence salvation) through good behavior. As Philip Yancey put it in a recent book on grace, "Grace baffles us because it goes against the intuition everyone has that, in the face of [our] injustice, some price must be paid. . . . By instinct [we] feel [we] must *do something* in order to be accepted."[11] A word picture may help us explain to an unbeliever that forgiveness is a gift of God's grace. Here's an example:

> Have you ever really hurt your spouse or girlfriend, and no matter what you did you couldn't get rid of the guilty feelings? You think if you send her flowers and candy, you'll feel better. But it doesn't work. You still feel an estrangement that you can't seem to shake. Finally one day, knowing your heart and sensing your guilt, she says, "You know, you don't need to keep trying to earn my forgiveness. I want you to know that there is nothing you can ever do that could earn my love. I forgave you the moment you hurt me because I love you. That's not something you can earn. It's something I give you. All you need to do is ask for my forgiveness and accept it. If I didn't love you, I

wouldn't forgive you, and all the presents and apologies in the world wouldn't change me."

Aren't word pictures the teaching technique Jesus employed most often? Jesus taught His greatest truths through stories and illustrations. Read, for example, the parables of the Unforgiven Servant in Matthew 18:21–35 and the Good Samaritan in Luke 10:25–37. These and other parables are word pictures drawn from the lessons and circumstances of everyday life. Jesus' purpose was to teach truths concerning the kingdom of God in a way that was relevant yet understandable to His audience. Parables served this purpose best.

Andres Tapia, associate editor for Pacific News Service, in an article titled "Reaching the First Post-Christian Generation," points out that today's "baby busters" (people born between 1963 and 1977) are increasingly rejecting "modernism" (the assumption that truth is rational and objective) in favor of "postmodernism" (truth is subjective and relative). "According to experts," he explains, "it is no longer enough to present the gospel's propositional truths." Rather,

> Experts say another communication device effective for reaching this generation is storytelling. Evangelist Leighton Ford . . . stresses the power of narrative preaching, particularly stories focused on Jesus. The use of personal stories where the teacher makes him or herself vulnerable is . . . an effective means of connecting with these young adults.[12]

Here's his point. There are people who are going to be more receptive to evangelistic techniques that employ emotive avenues rather than "propositional truths." Our personal testimonies, movies such as the *Jesus* film, and fiction novels all fall under the broad category of "word pictures."

I strongly suspect that, if our country continues along the postmodern path, future apologetics will need to utilize religious experiences and narrative stories as a means to convey Christian truths. It will be a case of adapting our witness to cultural trends.

Endnotes

1. Jim Petersen, *Evangelism As a Lifestyle* (Colorado Springs: Navpress, 1984), 88.
2. Peter Kreeft and Ronald K. Tacelli, *Handbook of Christian Apologetics* (Downers Grove, Ill.: InterVarsity, 1994), 23.
3. *Connexions: Developing a Lifestyle of Evangelism Among Friends* (Ellicott City, Md.: Search Ministries, 1994), 38.
4. Ibid., 78.
5. Petersen, *Evangelism As a Lifestyle*, 110.
6. C. S. Lewis, *God in the Dock* (Grand Rapids: Eerdmans, 1970), 256–57.
7. Dan Story, *Christianity on the Offense* (Grand Rapids: Kregel, 1998), chap. 12.
8. Millard J. Erickson, *Postmodernizing the Faith: Evangelical Responses to the Challenge of Postmodernism* (Grand Rapids: Baker, 1998), 89.
9. Nick Pollard, *Evangelism Made Slightly Less Difficult: How to Interest People Who Aren't Interested* (Downers Grove, Ill.: InterVarsity, 1997), 70.
10. Gary Smalley and John Trent, *The Language of Love* (Pomona, Calif.: Focus on the Family, 1988), 9.
11. Philip Yancey, *What's So Amazing About Grace?* (Grand Rapids: Zondervan, 1997), 67, 71.
12. Andres Tapia, "Reaching the First Post-Christian Generation," *Christianity Today*, 12 September 1994, 21.

6

Points of Contact

According to pollster George Barna's survey of religious views in America,

> [M]ost Americans possess perspectives on life and spirituality that conform to an orthodox Christian view of the world. Most Americans claim that the Bible is God's Word and is totally accurate in what it teaches.... [A] majority of nonbelievers said that both religion and the Bible were very important in their lives today. This is not exactly evidence of spiritual revival. But it suggests an environment in which a reasonable discussion of religious thought and a rational display of religious practice is wholly acceptable, if not desirable.[1]

This statement is encouraging in terms of its relevance to evangelism. Barna is saying that most Americans still identify, at least culturally, with Christianity. Of course, as we saw in chapter one, many of these people are not committed Christians, nor are they necessarily saved. But, as Barna observes, at *least* they identify with Christianity. This creates an environment that is highly favorable to evangelism and Christian apologetics. Most people are willing to discuss spiritual issues—even from a Christian perspective.

The problem we want to explore in this chapter is how to initiate a "reasonable discussion" with an unbeliever concerning the authenticity of Christianity and the life-transforming power of Jesus Christ. Our present task will be to examine an effective way of doing this through points of contact.

f Contact

Points of contact are apologetic springboards. They focus on topics that concern both Christians and non-Christians alike. Hence, they are starting points of conversation, common denominators, and areas of mutual agreement from which religious and ethical discussions can blossom. Let me illustrate this.

Most people, including most atheists, accept the fact that Jesus is a historical person—He really lived. However, non-Christians usually think of Him as merely a "good" man—a religious teacher, a great prophet, or a holy man—not God incarnate. But at least they do acknowledge that He lived.

This is a point of contact. It's an area of mutual agreement that can lead to a discussion of just *who Jesus Christ is.* We agree that He exists, but what is He really like? Did Jesus actually claim to be God? If Jesus was merely a "good" man, would He have made this claim? Certainly if Jesus wasn't God, claiming to be God would not make Him good—it would make him a liar or a lunatic! He can't be good if he's a liar or lunatic. If Jesus wasn't God, He would have to be one or the other. But is there any evidence that Jesus is a liar or lunatic? On the other hand, is there evidence that He's God? If so, what is that evidence? Can it be checked out?

Let me put this as a dialogue. Notice I'm using the Socratic Method.

Believer:	"We both agree that Jesus lived, so who do you think He is?"
Unbeliever:	"I think he was a famous moral teacher. You know, a great man. Perhaps even a prophet."
Believer:	"Tell me, would a moral teacher or a great man or a prophet be a liar?"
Unbeliever:	"Of course not."
Believer:	"So we can rule out Jesus being a liar?"
Unbeliever:	"Yes."
Believer:	"Good. Then let me ask you this. Do you think Jesus is a lunatic, that He was mentally deranged and just thought He was God?"
Unbeliever:	"Well, I suppose that could be true. I wouldn't think so, but it's possible."
Believer:	"What are the characteristics of a lunatic?"
Unbeliever:	"I guess erratic behavior, unpredictability, over-

	inflated ego, strange habits, strange ideas. I see what you're driving at. Jesus apparently didn't have these characteristics either."
Believer:	"Then what's left? If Jesus isn't a liar or a lunatic, and if he claimed to be God, who is He?"
Unbeliever:	"According to your argument, I guess He's God. But I still find it hard to believe."
Believer:	"I agree it is hard to believe. So why don't we go to His biography and look up some of the things He did and said. I think you'll come away convinced."

You see, the purpose of a point of contact is to get an unbeliever to consider the Christian perspective on the subject at hand. If we begin a witnessing encounter from an area of common ground, a point of mutual agreement in the area of religion or ethics, such as an idea, a concept, a principle, or a historical fact, we are far more likely to maintain a spirit of open-mindedness than if we plunge in, making blatant declarations ("The Bible clearly teaches that Jesus is God!") or criticizing the unbeliever's opinion ("You don't want to hear the facts").

When people agree with some foundational point under discussion—such as the historicity of Jesus Christ—we have taken the first step toward leading the conversation into a fuller revelation of the Christian position on any issue.

How They Work

Some theologians insist there is no common ground between believers and unbelievers. In mankind's fallen state, they claim an unbridgeable chasm exists between redeemed Christians and estranged unbelievers, a difference so severe that any meaningful dialogue in the area of spiritual truth is impossible. Unbelievers don't want to hear the Christian message, and even if they did, they would not understand it—let alone accept it.

I disagree. The fact is, Christians and non-Christians can and do engage in religious discussions that can and do result in religious conversions. If this were not possible, evangelism would be futile, and Christ's mandate to be His witnesses "in Jerusalem, and in all Judea and Samaria, and to the ends of the earth" (Acts 1:8) would not only be meaningless but baffling.

Theologian Alister McGrath explains this concept well:

> [S]ecular and Christian rationalities, although dis-
> tinct, overlap at points. Sin has a noetic influence
> in that it disrupts the continuity between secular
> and Christian outlooks; it does not, however, de-
> stroy their contiguity. The task of the apologist is
> to identify the areas of overlap in order to facili-
> tate the transition from a secular to a Christian
> worldview.
>   It is thus possible to make the transition from a
> secular to a Christian outlook through the points of
> contact that act as bridges between the two. There
> is not so much a "no man's land," as an area of
> shared possibilities, a region in which there is room
> for ambiguity. The creative apologist will direct
> attention to this region with a view to exploring it
> and emerging within the context of a Christian
> worldview. This region could prove the vital bridge
> between a secular and Christian worldview,
> enabling someone previously committed to the
> former to make the critical transition to the latter.[2]

McGrath observes that *"a point of contact is a God-given foothold
for divine self-revelation"* (emphasis mine).[3] In other words, God
Himself provides points of contact. He does this by instilling in
all people everywhere, by virtue of their creation in His image
(Gen. 1:26), basic moral, spiritual, psychological, social, creative,
aesthetic, physical, and emotional needs and capabilities. All of
these are "divine self-revelation" in that their ultimate source can
only be God. Hence, they point to God. For example, both Christians and non-Christians possess an intuitive understanding of
what constitutes proper moral behavior (Rom. 2:15). Both rely on
God-given principles of logic to make heads or tails of reality.
Most importantly, both Christians and non-Christians share
(whether acknowledged or not) an innate, created awareness that
God exists (see Rom. 1:19).
    The presence of these universal human traits and yearnings
explains why pantheists and monotheists have different concepts

of God, but both agree He exists. It explains why Muslims and Christians differ in their relationship with God, but share common spiritual needs. It explains why theists and atheists disagree on whether God even exists, yet use the same principles of logic to govern their conclusions. It also explains why all cultures, regardless of their worldviews, appreciate beauty, exhibit God-given creative powers through art and music, and endorse selflessness, bravery, and wisdom while condemning selfishness, cowardice, and stupidity.[4]

The fact is, people everywhere share fundamental notions of what constitutes reality in terms of what is essential to fulfilling basic human physical, emotional, and spiritual needs. For this reason, evangelism can be successful among diverse worldviews that foster different customs, religions, and languages.

Points of contact, however, are not ends in themselves. As McGrath says, they are bridges between a secular and a Christian worldview. They serve the purpose of bringing Christians and non-Christians together at a point of mutual agreement. But apologetics must be applied to further the evangelistic task. As McGrath explains:

> Points of contact are not in themselves adequate to bring people into the kingdom of God. They are merely *starting points.* Nor are they adequate in themselves to bring people to a specifically *Christian* faith. They might well point toward the existence of a creative and benevolent supreme being. The connection with "the God and Father of our Lord Jesus Christ" (1 Peter 1:3) remains to be made. The apologist must still show that the Christian gospel is consistent with these points of contact, that it is able to explain them, and more than that it is able to deliver all that they promise, turning hints into reality.[5]

The primary purpose of this book has been to teach the reader how to apply apologetics once an initial point of contact has been established. In the scenario above, after the point of contact had been made, apologetics came into play through a series of Socratic questions designed to reveal the real Jesus Christ. Had the unbeliever refused to examine Scripture at the end of the discussion, we would have identified the reason and returned to apologetics (or applied law—see chap. 1). Points of contact are used to gain a willing audience. Apologetics, gospel, or law must be applied to complete the evangelistic task.

Biblical Examples

The apostle Paul had to deal with many of the same obstacles to faith that we do today. There were no Mormons or Muslims in first-century Palestine, but there were many other competing religions and philosophical worldviews. In some cases, Paul witnessed directly from Scripture. The Bible was his point of contact. In other encounters, the Bible couldn't be used. Here are a few examples.

In Acts 17:2–3 Luke writes, "As his custom was, Paul went into the synagogue, and on three Sabbath days he reasoned with them from the Scriptures, explaining and proving that the Christ had to suffer and rise from the dead."

In this instance, Paul used the Bible (the Hebrew Old Testament) as a point of contact with the Jews in Thessalonica. Like Paul, they accepted Scripture as the Word of God. Hence, the Bible was Paul's "foot in the door," and some Jews became Christians because he was able to demonstrate from Scripture that Jesus was the divine Messiah (the "Christ," v. 3).

Likewise, we can use the Bible as a point of contact today, not only with Jewish people, but also with Jehovah's Witnesses and other cultists who (more or less) accept the Bible as divine revelation.

In Acts 14:15–17 Paul used a different point of contact. In this passage Paul and Barnabas were witnessing to the Gentiles in Lystra. His point of contact was "general revelation" in creation (see Rom. 1:19–20). The Gentiles in Lystra were pagans. They would not have been familiar with—or likely to accept—the Hebrew Old Testament as a point of contact. But apparently they did recognize the presence of the divine in nature. So Paul pointed out that,

> the living God . . . made heaven and earth and sea
> and everything in them. . . . Yet he has not left him-
> self without testimony: He has shown kindness by

> giving you rain from heaven and crops in their sea-
> sons; he provides you with plenty of food and fills
> your hearts with joy.

Paul used still another point of contact in Acts 26:1–3. Here the apostle defends himself before Herod Agrippa. Paul appeals to Agrippa's knowledge of the Jews and their customs. Beginning in verse 2 he says:

> King Agrippa, I consider myself fortunate to stand
> before you today as I make my defense against all
> the accusations of the Jews, and especially so be-
> cause you are well acquainted with all the Jewish
> customs and controversies. Therefore, I beg you to
> listen to me patiently.

By far the most explicit and well-developed examples of Paul establishing points of contact are found in Acts 17:16–31 where he confronts the Greek philosophers before the Areopagus. We will look at this remarkable account in detail because it's a splendid illustration of skilled apologetic tactics springing from initial points of contact.[6]

Paul was in Athens waiting for Silas and Timothy to arrive from Thessalonica (vv.13–16). Not one to be idle, Paul "reasoned in the synagogue with the Jews and the God-fearing Greeks, as well as in the marketplace day by day with those who happened to be there" (v. 17).

No doubt it was in the marketplace that some of the Epicurean and Stoic philosophers heard Paul's preaching and invited him to explain this "new teaching" before the Areopagus who met on Mar's Hill. The Areopagus was a council responsible for evaluating the morality and teachings of those who lectured in public places, as Paul was doing (kind of a "philosophy police"). Paul used this as an opportunity to evangelize the Greek philosophers.

While exploring the city of Athens, Paul noticed that the Greeks worshiped a host of pagan gods. Their idols and numerous altars were widespread throughout the city (v. 16). One particular altar carried the inscription, "TO AN UNKNOWN GOD" (v. 23). Perhaps the Greeks were concerned that they might overlook a particular god and erected this altar to cover, so to speak, all their bases. In any event, this altar to the unknown god became Paul's first point of contact.

Paul's discourse rested on the assumption—one that the Greeks would agree with (thus making the assumption a point of contact)—that all people possess a sense of the divine. Everyone intuitively knows that God exists, even if they don't know the one true God (see Eccl. 3:11; Rom. 1:19).

Paul applied this point of contact by acknowledging that the Athenians were "very religious" people (Acts 17:22) as shown by their many idols and altars. In other words, they too recognized the presence of the divine. He then zeroed in on the altar to the unknown god and pointed out that this God is in fact the one true God. Here he employed a second point of contact: The God whom the Greeks knew nothing about is the real God.

Having gotten the philosophers' attention through two points of contact, Paul continued by explaining what God is like. He described Him in general terms as the Creator, and as a God who does not inhabit shrines made with human hands (v. 24). Furthermore, this God is not dependent upon the ministrations of people since it is He who gives life to all creatures and who is sovereign over all the nations of the world (vv. 25–26).

Next, Paul pointed out that the reason God has revealed Himself through creation and His sovereignty over all the nations is so that people everywhere would seek Him out and find Him. God is not far, Paul added, from anyone (v. 27).

Then Paul did a remarkable thing. Rather than quote biblical passages to confirm this (remember, the Hebrew Bible was probably foreign to the Greeks), he quoted from two of their own pagan poets: the Cretan poet Epimendides who said, "For in him we live and move and have our being," and the Cilician poet Aratus who said, "For we are his offspring" (v. 28).

Now just what was Paul doing here? Paul recognized that quoting biblical passages to confirm his message would mean nothing to the Greeks. They weren't familiar with the Hebrew Scripture and would certainly not accept it as authoritative. So Paul employed a third point of contact: he appealed to their own pagan poets.

In other words, Paul used *secular (non-biblical) evidence* to confirm biblical truths. He realized that even the pagan poets maintained a limited apprehension of the one true God—despite the fact that this knowledge had degenerated into horrendous pagan worship (see Rom. 1:18–32).

Finally, in Acts 17:29 and following, Paul shifted from apologetics to preaching. Having gained an attentive audience by employing three points of contact, he moved to the heart of his message. If this "unknown" God is in fact the one true God, then the other gods worshiped by the Greeks, as represented by their idols, are false gods. Moreover, like all people, the Greeks are responsible to the God who created them and who is sovereign over their lives. Therefore people will be judged according to their response to Him. (Notice that Paul is preaching law.)

This is especially so, Paul continued, because God has now revealed Himself clearly and specifically in the person of Jesus Christ. That Jesus speaks the words of God is confirmed by His resurrection from the dead (v. 31). (Notice that Paul has now switched from law to gospel.)

Let me recap these passages. Paul applied three points of contact that he knew the Greeks would acknowledge as true without further discussion: their innate sense of the divine; the existence of a God whom they did not know; and their own poets who, even if unwittingly, recognized that God is the source of life and breath—the Creator of all things. Building on these points of contact, Paul presented an evangelistic message that resulted in some of the Greeks becoming Christians and an open door for the spread of the gospel in Athens (v. 34).

Now I want you to notice three things in the passages we examined. First, Paul didn't depend on his personal testimony or a first-century version of the "Four Spiritual Laws" as the basis of his evangelism. Rather, he used techniques of apologetics. To reach the Jews in Thessalonica, Paul "reasoned" from Scripture in the synagogue (also see Acts 19:8). To reach the Gentiles in Lystra, he presented external evidence from creation (general revelation). In the case of King Agrippa, he applied logical reasoning based on common knowledge. And before the Greek philosophers, Paul relied, in part, on secular sources.

Second, when Paul witnessed to the Jews, Gentiles, and Greek philosophers, his goal was to lead his hearers to Jesus Christ—as all good apologetics does. He did not merely engage in intellectual debating.

Third, Paul was familiar with the Greek poets. He didn't get this information reading his Bible or attending rabbinical schools. He obviously spent time becoming familiar with the Greek religions in order to witness more effectively. Paul did his homework, and he used apologetics.

Paul was an effective evangelist because he was willing to accommodate what unbelievers believe—without compromising truth—as points of contact in order to gain a hearing for the gospel. Paul knew that an initial point of contact is crucial if witnessing is to proceed.

In 1 Corinthians 9:19–22 Paul gives the clarion call of apologetics:

> Though I am free and belong to no man, I make myself a slave to everyone, to win as many as possible. To the Jews I became like a Jew, to win the Jews. To those under the law I became like one under the law (though I myself am not under the law), so as to win those under the law. To those not having the law [Gentiles] I became like one not having the law (though I am not free from God's law but am under Christ's law), so as to win those not having the law. To the weak I became weak, to win the weak. I have become all things to all men so that by all possible means I might save some.

A Few Examples

Below are ten sample points of contact—areas of mutual agreement between Christians and non-Christians—that can be used to initiate conversations. All of them open doors to congenial, thought-provoking discussions on subjects of importance to both.[7]

Nature. Many unbelievers claim they feel the presence of God in nature. This is a point of contact. We explain why the God they sense in nature and the God of Scripture are one and the same. God created nature and is revealed in His creation (Ps. 8; Rom. 1:20).

Morality. All people, in all cultures, and throughout all of history—in spite of differences in languages, customs, and religions—maintain a similar understanding of right and wrong behavior. This points to a moral Lawgiver who has placed in the minds of all people an instinctive moral conscience (Rom. 2:14–15).

Spiritual yearnings. Most people believe in a deity and crave a relationship with God. Atheism is an anomaly—people learn to disbelieve in God. This is because God has placed an innate awareness of Himself in the hearts and minds of all people (Rom. 1:19). This opens the door for a discussion of "What is God like?" and the fact that only Christianity can offer objective evidence that it is God's sole revelation.

Here's another way to look at it. Non-Christian worldviews are not totally false in all their components. All worldviews contain elements of truth—even spiritual truth. Now don't misunderstand me; I'm not saying that non-Christian religions lead to God. But I am saying that, through general revelation, many religions do contain ingredients of truth, and these areas of light afford points of contact. We can acknowledge our agreement at these points, show their similarity with Christian teachings, and then move on to their fuller revelation in Scripture.

Aesthetics. The family of humankind shares an appreciation of beauty and a love of art, music, and literature. This is a result of being created in the image of God; it is our God-given capacity to create, a reflection of the God who created us. This too can lead to a discussion of the nature of God.

Sin. Almost all fiction books and movies focus on the perpetual battle between good and evil forces. Likewise, all people struggle against lust, selfishness, greed, and pride. Thousands of years of civilization have not tempered this urge. Explore this propensity toward sin with unbelievers. How did it become ingrained in the human race? What is the remedy?

Suffering and evil. Everyone agrees that pain and suffering are real. Many people blame God or reject Him because He doesn't stop it. So we challenge unbelievers to remove God from the equation. What's the solution to suffering and evil if God doesn't exist?

Science. Most people trust science to reveal accurate truth. However, miracles and spiritual truth-claims (e.g., salvation through Jesus Christ alone) can't be ruled out by science because they are issues that fall beyond the scope of science to investigate. This can lead to a discussion of the evidences supporting God's existence and the Bible as God's Word.

Ethics. Christians agree that Christianity has its dark pages. Yet the same ethical standards by which critics judge the dark pages of Christianity have their source in the Bible. Challenge unbelievers to account for this. How can they endorse Christian ethics and still deny the Christian God? Consider how moral behavior is rapidly degenerating as Christianity loses its influence in society. Why is this?

Social services. Hospitals, orphanages, relief organizations, and universities are vital components of modern society. All of these have their source in the Christian church. What have atheistic governments contributed that have bettered humanity? At best, they have appropriated institutions Christianity began.

Fear of death. Everyone dies, and most people harbor a fear of death. What happens after death? Is there a better place waiting for us in the hereafter? How do we get there? Secular humanism and naturalism deny a future life. Pantheism and New Age beliefs offer only extinction (absorption). Other religions and cults promote views of salvation that can't be substantiated (such as becoming "gods" ourselves). Why not examine the Bible? It *can* be checked out and verified.

I'm not suggesting that these points of contact will automatically lead to a gospel presentation—or that unbelievers will be unable to muster counterarguments. The point is to engage in dialogue that allows us to explain the Christian perspective on issues and to offer an apologetic defense of our views.

Remember, Christianity is truth. If we have done our homework, we will successfully defend our positions against counterarguments.

Endnotes

1. George Barna, *The Barna Report, 1992–1993* (Ventura, Calif.: Regal, 1992), 21, 27.
2. Alister McGrath, *Intellectuals Don't Need God, and Other Modern Myths* (Grand Rapids: Zondervan, 1993), 57, 59.
3. Ibid., 16.
4. C. S. Lewis demonstrates this fact in his book, *The Abolition of Man* (New York: Macmillan, 1947).
5. McGrath, *Intellectuals Don't Need God,* 16.
6. For an excellent study of this passage see F. F. Bruce, *The Defense of the Gospel in the New Testament* (Grand Rapids: Eerdmans, 1977), 39–49.
7. The Christian perspective on most of these subjects can be found in my book *Defending Your Faith* (Grand Rapids: Kregel, 1997).

7

The Bottom Line

A year out of high school, one of my best friends became a Christian. At the time this was rather amazing to me, considering that religion was as far from our thoughts in the early 1960s as computers and video movies. Shortly after his conversion, he enrolled in seminary and moved out of state. Meanwhile, I got married and dropped out of college.

After graduating from seminary my friend returned home with his new bride to serve as a pastor in a local church. Although we had little in common by then, we got together one evening. I remember nothing of the conversation that ensued except for one comment that he made: "Even if my beliefs turn out to be wrong, being a Christian is still the best way to live."

Years later I became a Christian. Shortly after my own conversion, I returned to college, eventually entering graduate school to study apologetics. There I met the works of Blaise Pascal, and I was reminded again of my friend's comment. Philosophically, it was very similar to "Pascal's Wager."

Pascal was a seventeenth-century French mathematician, physicist, and theologian. He is best known in the area of apologetics for a compilation of his notes, published posthumously as *Pensées*. There one finds his famous wager.

Pascal believed that there are no rational grounds for belief in God, so it is futile for people to attempt to "reason" their way to Him.[1] In spite of this seemingly uncertain situation, Pascal claimed that people still had to choose to believe God exists or to believe He doesn't exist. But the choice is not one of reason. Like the flip of a coin, it was a fifty-fifty chance whether or not God exists.

Now, in spite of the fact that there is no guarantee that you are making the correct decision, Pascal argued that we must wager in favor of God because we have nothing to lose and everything to gain. Here's how Pascal put his wager:

> Let us weigh up the gain and the loss, in taking heads that God exists. Let us weigh these two cases: if you gain, you gain all; if you lose, you lose nothing. Wager then that he is, without hesitation.[2]

In other words, if God exists we win and have eternal bliss in heaven. But if God doesn't exist and we lose, we've actually lost nothing because there's nothing to lose. On the other hand, to wager against God is foolish because if God *does* exist we've lost everything because we lose eternal life. So the prudent person will always wager that God exists rather than to risk eternal suffering.

Pascal's Wager is not, of course, evidential apologetics. Like Kreeft and Tacelli in their book *Handbook of Christian Apologetics*, I "mention [the Wager] here . . . not because it is a proof for the existence of God, but because it can help us in our search for God in the absence of such proof."[3]

The authors continue their comments:

> The Wager can seem offensively venal and purely selfish. But it can be reformulated to appeal to a higher moral motive: If there is a God of infinite goodness, and he justly deserves my allegiance and faith, I risk doing the greatest injustice by not acknowledging him.
>
> The Wager cannot—or should not—coerce belief. But it can be an incentive for us to search for God, to study and restudy the arguments that seek to show that there is Something—or Someone—who is the ultimate explanation of the universe and of my life.[4]

I believe Pascal's Wager is a persuasive argument in the sense that it clearly reveals that there are only two options. Either choose

God and (at the very worse) lose nothing, or reject God and (at the very best) lose everything.

Fortunately, the evidence for God's existence and the reality of Christianity as His sole avenue of revelation, is more than a fifty-fifty chance. The overwhelming preponderance of evidence confirms Christianity—while at the same time it refutes non-Christian religions. Indeed, it's the accumulated strength of the evidence for Christianity that makes the odds in the wager unquestionably in favor of God. It's not a fifty-fifty chance.

The key to evidential apologetics, then, is its cumulative power. Clark Pinnock puts this in a useful word picture:

> If we think in terms of a rope, we notice that it is composed of strands of twine of various lengths and tensions. If we were to unravel it and test the strength of the strands separately, we would not find any of them unbreakable. Some of them might even be rather weak. But when the strands are bound together in the network we call a rope, the result is very strong indeed. The strength of the rope exceeds the sum of the strength of the strands individually. The strength of the argument for Christianity is found, not on one argument set off by itself but in the binding together of many evidences which conspire to produce strong conviction and a convincing basis for faith.[5]

Moreover, as Pinnock continues: "The evidences that speak for the Christian message are publicly accessible and I believe impressive."[6] Anyone can check them out.

The fact is, we need no more proof of the Christian message than God has given. Even if God provided more explicit evidence than He does—say, dramatic miracles such as those in Moses' day—it would still not convince some people to turn their lives over to Him. In the story of Lazarus and the rich man (Luke 16:19–31), the rich man, who finds himself in hell, argues that "if someone from the dead goes to [his five brothers], they will repent" (v. 30). But the reply is, "If they do not listen to Moses and the Prophets [God's Word], neither will they be persuaded if someone rises from the dead" (v. 31). Isn't this exactly what Jesus did? He rose from the dead to prove his deity (Rom. 1:4) and that He is Savior of the world (Acts 17:31). Yet people persist in rejecting Him.

Enough evidence is available to convince even the most relentless skeptic who's willing to go with the facts. But no amount of evidence will convince someone who is determined to resist God. The evidence is there, but, ultimately, the decision to accept Jesus as Lord and Savior is a moral and willful decision. Astrophysicist Hugh Ross illustrates this well:

> Several months ago I spoke at a prestigious American university to a group of about forty science professors. I presented much of the information that appears in the pages of this book [The Creator and the Cosmos]. Afterward, I conversed with four physics professors and asked their response.
>
> One of the four said he could not deny the truth of my message. The others nodded in agreement. I asked if they could see, then, the rationality of turning over their lives to Jesus Christ. Another of the four spoke up, saying, yes, they could see it, but they weren't yet ready to be that rational.
>
> This statement was not a brush-off. Each man went on to name his reasons for resistance. One confessed his unwillingness to give up sexual immorality. The others spoke of deep wounds inflicted long ago by people who called themselves Christians.[7]

When all is said and done, it seems to me that the bottom line is this: It is beyond reasonable doubt that Jesus Christ is exactly who He claims to be—the God-man Savior of the world. When the evidence is examined, and religious worldviews are compared, Christianity is unquestionably the only sustainable and verifiable option. Yet the final decision to become a Christian is necessarily a subjective one. A step of faith. Faith grounded on fact, but faith nevertheless.

You can look at it like this. There is a gap between probability and absolute certainty that must be bridged by faith. As Pascal clearly pointed out, the alternative to taking this step of faith is to risk eternal separation from God—a fate far worse that death itself. If Christianity is true, it must be embraced because there is no other option.

After a difficult teaching, many of Jesus' followers left (John 6:22–66). Jesus then asked His twelve disciples if they too would leave Him (v. 67). Peter responded with perhaps the wisest words ever uttered: "Lord, to whom shall we go? You have words of eternal life" (v. 68).

Still, as Pascal reminds us, the choice remains—God or unbelief. We have a free will and can choose either one.

Apologetics provides evidence to ground this faith decision. But it is like the proverbial, "You can lead a horse to water, but you can't make him drink." The evidence is there, but no one can make you accept it.

If doubts remain, let me suggest that you pray the skeptics prayer: "God, I don't know whether you exist or not, but if you do, please show me who you are."[8] Confess your doubts to God. The father of a boy who was demon possessed asked Jesus if He would take pity on his son and him. Jesus replied, "Everything is possible for him who believes." The boy's father immediately responded: "I do believe; help me overcome my unbelief!" (Mark 9:22–24).

There is nothing wrong with doubts. And God wants to remove your doubts. If you sincerely want to know God, pray to Him. Confess your doubts. Ask Him: "God, if you exist, reveal Yourself to me, confirm it in my heart." God will hear that prayer. As Pascal says, you have nothing to lose. But I'll "wager" that if you sincerely want to believe in God, and if you sincerely want a relationship with Him, He'll answer that prayer. Jesus said, "Ask and it will be given to you; seek and you will find; knock and the door will be opened to you. For everyone who asks receives; he who seeks finds; and to him who knocks, the door will be opened" (Matt. 7:7–8). The apostle Paul adds that God wishes all people to seek and find Him, and that He "is not far from each one of us" (Acts 17:27).

Life without God is doomed to failure. Life with a false god is doomed to failure. Inevitable and eternal punishment awaits both wrong choices: "The LORD searches every heart and understands every motive behind the thoughts. If you seek [God], he will be found by you; but if you forsake him, *he will reject you forever"* (1 Chron. 28:9, emphasis added). Take Pascal's Wager. Bet on God.

Endnotes

1. Norman Geisler, *Christian Apologetics* (Grand Rapids: Baker, 1987), 48.
2. Edward John Carnell, *An Introduction to Christian Apologetics* (Grand Rapids: Eerdmans, 1952), 358.
3. Peter Kreeft and Ronald K. Tacelli, *Handbook of Christian Apologetics* (Downers Grove, Ill.: InterVarsity, 1994), 85.
4. Ibid., 86.
5. Clark H. Pinnock, *Reason Enough: A Case for the Christian Faith* (Downers Grove, Ill.: InterVarsity, 1980), 120.
6. Ibid.
7. Hugh Ross, *The Creator and the Cosmos* (Colorado Springs: Navpress, 1993), 153.
8. Kreeft and Tacelli, *Handbook of Christian Apologetics*, 86.